TWAYNE'S WORLD LEADERS SERIES

EDITOR OF THIS VOLUME
Samuel Smith, Ph.D.

Friedrich Froebel

TWLS 74

Friedrich Froebel

FRIEDRICH FROEBEL

By ROBERT B. DOWNS

University of Illinois

TWAYNE PUBLISHERS

A DIVISION OF G. K. HALL & CO., BOSTON

Copyright © 1978 by G. K. Hall & Co.
All Rights Reserved
First Printing

Library of Congress Cataloging in Publication Data

Downs, Robert Bingham, 1903 -
  Friedrich Froebel.

  (Twayne's world leaders series; TWLS 74)
  Bibliography: p. 119 - 24
  Includes index.
  1. Froebel, Friedrich Wilhelm August, 1782 - 1852.
2. Teachers—Germany—Biography. 3. Education—
Philosophy. I. Title.
LB638.D68   370'.92'4 [B]   77 - 13512
ISBN 0-8057-7668-0

Contents

Preface

A true revolution in the world of elementary education was inspired by a quadrumvirate of nineteenth-century leaders—two Europeans and two Americans.

Beginning with Heinrich Pestalozzi in Switzerland and Friedrich Froebel in Germany and continuing with Horace Mann and Henry Barnard in the United States, a complete transformation of education for the very young occurred. Concepts and practices which had prevailed over the centuries for the instruction of children in their beginning years were rejected, as more enlightened forces took over.

Friedrich Froebel, the subject of the present biography, may rightfully be called the father of the kindergarten. His educational views have continued to exert a world-wide influence for well over a century, though of course modified with the passage of time by later research in the fields of education and psychology. Like other great pioneers, he blazed the trail for others to follow in building a broad highway.

Friedrich Froebel is the fourth volume on great educators in Twayne's World Leaders Series by the present author. The first three were *Horace Mann* (1974), *Heinrich Pestalozzi* (1975), and *Henry Barnard* (1977).

Appreciation should be expressed to Elizabeth C. Downs for her aid in research for this work and to Deloris Holiman for her assistance in the preparation of the manuscript.

ROBERT B. DOWNS

University of Illinois

Chronology

1782	Born April 21 at Oberweissbach in the Thuringian Forest, state of Schwartzburg-Rudolstadt.
1783	Death of mother.
1792 - 1797	Sent to live with uncle, Superintendent Hoffman, at Stadt Ilm.
1797 - 1799	Goes to Neuhaus in the Thuringian Forest as a forester's apprentice.
1799 - 1801	Student at Jena University.
1801 - 1805	Holds various posts: student of agriculture at Hildburghausen, actuary in a forestry department, land surveyor, secretary, and accountant at a large country estate.
1802	Death of father.
1805 - 1807	Goes to Frankfurt to study architecture, but instead becomes a teacher in Gruener's model school. Pays first visit to Pestalozzi's school at Yverdon, in August, 1805.
1807	Becomes tutor to sons of Herr von Holzhausen and wife.
1808 - 1810	Takes his pupils to Yverdon to study with Pestalozzi.
1810	Returns to Frankfurt.
1811	Becomes student at Göttingen University.
1812	Goes to University of Berlin to study crystallography under Weiss.
1813 - 1814	Joins Prussian volunteer corps in war of liberation against Napoleon's forces.
1814 - 1816	Returns to Berlin as assistant in the mineralogical museum, University of Berlin.
1816	Establishes "Universal German Educational Institution" at Griesheim in Rudolstadt.
1817	Transfers school to Keilhau, where he is joined by Heinrich Langethal and Wilhelm Middendorff, wartime associates.
1818	Marries Wilkelmine Hoffmeister.
1826	Publishes *The Education of Man*.

1828	Johannes Barop, Middendorff's nephew, joins Educational Community at Keilhau.
1829	Prepares plan for a National Educational Institute in Helba to submit to Duke of Meiningen. Plan abandoned two years later for lack of support.
1831	Goes to Frankfurt and then to Wartensee in Lucerne and opens a school.
1832	Accepts invitation to transfer school to Willisau in Lucerne.
1835	Accepts direction of school and orphanage for canton of Berne at Bergdorf.
1836	Leaves Switzerland to return to Rudolstadt.
1837	Opens an institute for the education of very young children at Blankenburg and begins to develop series called "gifts and occupations."
1838 - 1840	Publishes articles in *Sunday Journal* on play material and travels to Dresden, Leipzig, and elsewhere to promote new movement.
1839	Death of wife.
1840	Names kindergarten and founds kindergartens at Blankenburg and Rudolstadt.
1843	Publishes *Mutter und Kose-lieder*.
1844 - 1847	Lectures in Dresden, Darmstadt, Hamburg, Heidelberg, Frankfurt.
1848	Attends teachers' conference called by him at Rudolstadt.
1849	Moves to Liebenstein near Eisenach to begin training of kindergarten teachers.
1850	Berthe von Marenholz-Bülow visits institution and begins lifelong support for the cause. Institution removed to Marienthal.
1851	Marries Luise Leven. Prussian government bans kindergartens.
1852	Dies on June 21 at Marienthal.

CHAPTER 1

Early Years

THAT the child is father to the man is amply demonstra-ted in the career of Friedrich Froebel, celebrated nineteenth-century German educator. The sometimes traumatic experiences of his early childhood were major influences in shaping Froebel's sub-sequent progress.

As related in his autobiography, Friedrich Wilhelm August Froe-bel was born on April 21, 1782, at Oberweissbach, a village in the Thuringian Forest, belonging to the small principality of Schwarzburg-Rudolstadt, Germany. His father was principal pastor of a district inhabited by some five thousand persons, scattered among six or seven villages, belonging to the Old Lutheran Protes-tant Church. The task of serving such a sizable number of parishioners, plus superintending the building of a large new church, was all-absorbing of the father's time, taking him away from home for extended periods so that he was unable to devote more than sporadic attention to his children.

Perhaps worn out by too frequent child-bearing, Friedrich's mother died when he was only nine months old, leaving five sons. Thus, the youngest child never knew his own mother. The fact is significant, for in later years, Friedrich glorified the concept of motherhood, creating in his imagination an ideal mother who is the central figure in one of his most famous books *Mother Songs and Games*, where she is virtually canonized as a saint. In the last period of his life, Froebel reverted to his infancy and erected a monument to the mother whom he was destined never to know.

In the absence of a mother—and for most practical purposes of a father—Friedrich's care fell principally on his older brothers and occasional servants. When Friedrich was about four years of age, his father remarried. "I remember," he wrote, "that I received my new mother overflowing with feelings of simple and faithful child-love

11

towards her. These sentiments made me happy, developed my nature, and strengthened me, because they were kindly received and reciprocated by her."[1]

But this blissful relationship did not long endure. With the birth of a son of her own, the stepmother's attention was wholly focused on the new infant. Thenceforth, she appears to have played to the hilt the proverbial role of the cruel stepmother. The sensitive four-year-old always carried the scar of the neglect suffered during that period of his life. As Froebel recollected, the stepmother's "love was not only withdrawn entirely from me and transferred to her own child, but I was treated with worse than indifference—by word and deed, I was made to feel an utter stranger."[2]

Under these circumstances, Friedrich spent an unhappy child-hood, a fact which caused him later to resolve to attempt to bring happiness to other children. He became introspective, emotional, mystic, and was regarded as "moonstruck." His father's efforts to teach him to read were frustrating to both teacher and pupil. His schooling was haphazard, he learned little, and soon gained the reputation of being stupid, mischievous, and untrustworthy. As a result, Friedrich began to hate school, church, and family, except for a favorite brother, Cristoph. Shut up in the gloomy parsonage most of the time, left to the care of a single housemaid, the child lacked playmates and playthings. The father and son seem never to have understood each other. On that point Froebel notes, "Although my father was a stirring, active man, seldom surpassed in his relations as country pastor, in education, learning and ex-perience, yet I remained a stranger to him through his entire life, owing to these separations caused by early circumstances."[3]

Depressing to a young child also was Froebel's home environ-ment. The house in which he was born was closely surrounded by other buildings, walls, hedges, and fences; and Friedrich was strict-ly forbidden to go beyond the yard and garden. Moments of relief from the monotony came when he helped his father with the gar-dening. Because the plant world fascinated him, the study of nature was thereafter a lifelong preoccupation, becoming an essential ele-ment in the kindergarten system when it was established by Froebel in his later years.

Because Froebel's father had an unfavorable opinion of the vil-lage boys' school, Friedrich was sent to the girls' school, contrary to standing rules. There he read the Bible with the older pupils and also learned the sacred songs which were sung on Sundays in the church. Certain of the hymns he found inspiring, both in his early childhood and in later life. Religion was a constant factor in the lives of the Froebel family. Divine services were held twice each Sunday, and Friedrich was seldom permitted to miss attending all such exercises. He followed his father's sermons with rapt attention, sitting apart from the rest of the congregation, in the vestry. Friedrich notes that his father belonged to the old orthodox school of theology, "and in consequence the language both of his hymns and of his sermons was mystical and symbolic"[4]—accounting perhaps for the son's later fondness for mystical and symbolic forms for the expression of his own ideas.

In the village school, only arithmetic came easily to Friedrich. He confesses that since learning to read was hard work for him, his father regarded him as a hopelessly stupid boy, unfitted for a university education. There was some basis for the harsh judgment. The ability to express himself adequately or gracefully in speech or in writing was always a stumbling block for Froebel. Grammar was a constant barrier, and his repeated efforts to learn Latin were unsuccessful.

As an occasional tutor, Friedrich's older brother Christoph was an inspiration to him. Christoph was a student in theology at the University of Jena and brought back new views which his father regarded as sheer heresy and damnable innovation. Friedrich listened enthralled to their hot discussions, even though the ideas were not all comprehensible to him. From Christoph, Friedrich learned sexual differences in plant life, opening up new vistas for him in the world of nature.

Friedrich also absorbed much knowledge of the ways of the world by listening to many interviews between his father and members of the pastor's flock. The young lad sat quietly and unobtrusively, reading a book, while visitors poured out their tales of distress and sought the minister's counsel. "But it was the dark side of life that was thus revealed to him," a contemporary writer noted. "It was the complaint of the sorely-tried mother over the ungrateful son, the acknowledgment of a hidden sin, a melancholy fall, it was the sting of conscience, fear, repentance, despair, which alternately had the word, while the earnest, yes, severe teacher, now through the inexorable precepts of the divine law, then with the consolations of mercy, strove to work on the dejected minds. These conversations and other influences of that time revealed to Friedrich the inner life of men, with its hidden springs and its concealed strife and pain, and he perceived more and more the connection between things and words and aims."[5]

In the autumn of 1792, a visitor came to the parsonage at Oberweissbach who took a deep interest in Friedrich Froebel, then age ten. This was a maternal uncle, Herr Hoffman, pastor at Stadt Ilm, a market town north of Froebel's home. Herr Hoffman had lost his own wife and child some years previously. The uncle, a gentle, affectionate man, resembled his sister in many ways; and he and his nephew were mutually attracted to each other. A proposal by Herr Hoffman that he should become his nephew's guardian, and be responsible for his care and education, was gladly accepted by Friedrich's father. For the next five years the boy led a free and happy life. He joined the upper class of the town school with forty school boys of his own age. As revealed in his *Autobiography*, "As austerity reigned in my father's house, so here kindness and benevolence. There I encountered mistrust; here I was trusted. There I was under restraint; here I had liberty. . . . My uncle's house had gardens attached, into which I could go if I liked; but I was also at liberty to roam through the whole region, provided I returned home punctually."[6]

In Friedrich's new school reading, writing, and arithmetic were well taught; and the religious instruction was excellent. Latin, he reported, "was miserably taught," and "in physical geography we repeated our tasks parrot-wise, speaking much and knowing nothing." Friedrich was deeply chagrined to find that, because of the previous lack of physical training and exercise, he had difficulty keeping up with the other boys in their games. Nevertheless, he gained freedom of mind and bodily strength day by day.

Soon after Friedrich's return to his father's home, at the age of fifteen, it was decided that he should serve a two-year apprenticeship with a forester, a surveyor and assessor living at Neuhaus, with the object of learning forestry, geometry, and land-surveying, in preparation for later becoming an agriculturist. Froebel writes, "I wanted to be an agriculturist in the full meaning of the word; for I loved mountain, field, and forest; and I heard also that to learn anything solid in this occupation one must be well acquainted with geometry and land-surveying."[7]

The apprenticeship to the forester did not prove entirely successful. Friedrich's master had learned his art through experience rather than by formal training; and though he was a man possessing wide practical knowledge, he was not a competent teacher. Furthermore, he was absent from home for long periods and had little time to devote to his assistant. As related in the *Autobiography*, Froebel's two years in the forest were spent in several ways. Aside from the day to day duties assigned to him, he studied the forester's "really excellent books on forestry and geometry," and spent time studying forest nature. A friendly doctor in a nearby town, who studied natural history as an avocation, loaned to him books on botany, from which he learned about plants other than those seen in the forest. Much time was spent also in making maps of the neighborhood. Botany enthralled him especially, to such an extent, he notes, that "My religious life now changed to a religious communion with nature, and in the last half-year I lived entirely amongst and with my plants, which drew me towards them and fascinated me. . . . Collecting and drying specimens of plants was a work I prosecuted with the greatest care."[8]

During these months, living in solitude, always surrounded by natural phenomena, with ample time for solitary reflection, Froebel began to perceive the unity and continuity of nature. At the same time, in recalling his own previous education, he felt that prevailing school methods were of slight value. These youthful conclusions directly influenced Froebel's later educational theories and practices.

In the course of Froebel's stay at Neuhaus, a company of strolling players presented a series of plays in a neighboring castle. After attending the first showing, he went again and again, recording that "these performances made a deep and lively impression upon me." He found inspiring the poetic nature of the dramas; on the hour's walk home in the dark or under the starry sky he recalled and lived over again the scenes of each play. When his father subsequently learned of his attendance at these performances, Friedrich was severely reprimanded for such frivolous, if not immoral, behavior.

The son, on the other hand, felt that he gained as much benefit from the play-going as from church attendance, in the way of moral uplift and self-culture.

A certain amount of unpleasantness accompanied the end of Friedrich's two-year apprenticeship to the forester. His master wished him to remain for a third year; and when he decided to return home instead, the forester wrote a critical letter to Friedrich's father, despite the fact that he had previously given the lad a "thoroughly satisfactory testimonial." Any excuses or explanations were ignored, for Friedrich states that "my father, at the beginning of my apprenticeship, had told me not to come to him with any complaint, as I should never be listened to, but should be considered as wrong beforehand."[9]

Another turning point came in young Friedrich's life soon after his return home, when it was arranged that he should serve as a messenger to carry some money to his brother Traugott, a medical student at the University of Jena. When Froebel reached the university town in the summer of 1799, he reported that he "was seized by the stirring intellectual life of the place, and I longed to remain there a little time." Eight weeks of the summer term remained. His father agreed to let Friedrich stay to study topographical and plan drawing. So stimulated was the lad by his brief encounter with a university community that he petitioned his father to allow him to continue at Jena as a regular student. The main obstacle was financial, but that block was removed by a small legacy left Friedrich by his mother. Thus, in 1799, at the age of seventeen-and-a-half, he entered the University of Jena as a fully matriculated student.

Friedrich's interests in the university curriculum appear to have been omnivorous, but with a decided bent for scientific and technical subjects. He states, "I heard lectures on applied mathematics, arithmetic, algebra, geometry, mineralogy, botany, natural history, physics, chemistry, accounts, cultivation of forest trees and management of forests, architecture, house-building and land surveying. I continued topographical drawing."[10] The teaching, no matter how excellent, had an important defect in Friedrich's view: the arrangement of courses was arbitrary, and there was no attempt to show their connection. Mathematical experiments were unsatisfying, for they seemed merely to demonstrate the obvious. "On the other hand," Froebel concedes, "my attention was riveted by the study of gravitation, of force, of weight, which were living things to me, because of their evident relation to actual facts." He adds, "Chemistry fascinated me. The excellent teacher always demonstrated the true connection of the phenomena under consideration; and the theory of chemical affinity took strong hold upon me."[11]

Botany, Froebel's favorite subject, was also well taught at Jena. His instructor in botany and natural history, Batsch, gave his students a clear understanding of nature as one whole; and as a result Froebel notes that his "love for the observation of Nature in detail became more animated." Two principles in particular, learned from Batsch, appealed to Froebel: first, "the conception of the mutual relationship of all animals, extending like a network in all directions; and the second that the skeleton or bony framework of fishes, birds, and men was one and the same in plan, and that the skeleton of man should be considered as the fundamental type which Nature strove to produce even in the lower forms of creation."[12] Froebel found great intellectual and spiritual satisfaction in the concept of the interconnection and unity of natural phenomena—ideas which were destined to be incorporated in his educational system.

Froebel's scientific studies, especially in the field of mineralogy, taught him the usefulness and importance of close observation. This experience, too, became a part of his later teaching methods, leading him to give little children directions and encouragement in how to see details of objects, inculcating in them habits of lifelong value.

The stay at Jena ended on a sour note for Froebel. He loaned part of his college fund to his brother Traugott, who left the university without repaying the loan. Friedrich's father refused further financial aid, and Friedrich, unwilling to abandon his studies, allowed eating-house bills to accumulate. Falling into debt was regarded as a crime, and soon young Froebel found himself in the university prison. Nine weeks passed before his father agreed to pay the price of having him released, and then only if Friedrich would sign a document giving up all claim to his rightful share in any future inheritance from his father's estate. These episodes are typical in fact of the poor business sense which characterized Froebel's entire life: lending money with no assurance of repayment, incurring debts beyond his ability to pay, and forfeiting his legacy.

Unwilling to face the shame of his prison record at Jena, Froebel returned home, discouraged and frustrated, at the age of nineteen. For a time, he busied himself with a study of German literature, becoming acquainted with the works of Schiller, Goethe, Wieland, and other writers in his father's library, though the collection was predominantly theological in nature. Another undertaking, as Froebel describes it, was "to make a collection of comprehensive extracts of scientific matters from the several periodicals received by my father." This enterprise was regarded by the father as a waste of time and paper. Nevertheless, Friedrich states that "indeed the work proved of actual service to me, for it brought a certain order, breadth, and firmness into my ideas which had the most beneficial effect upon men."[13]

For the next four years, Froebel drifted from job to job, trying to find himself. Some of his father's relatives had farm property near Hildburghausen, managed by a steward. Friedrich was sent there to study practical farming under the steward's direction and took part in all the ordinary occupations. It did not take him long, however, to realize that he had no particular liking for or inclination toward agriculture and that this career would be unsuitable for him.

While thus engaged, Friedrich was called home because of his father's serious illness. The father and son were completely reconciled before the father died in February, 1802. At Easter time in the same year, Froebel left the parsonage at Oberweissbach, with the last of his home ties cut. There is no record that he ever returned there, certainly not for any extended stay. Henceforth he was the master of his own actions.

Still uncertain of his future career, Froebel's first position after departure from his father's home was in Bamberg, where he remained for a year as a clerk in the Office of Woods and Forest. He notes that "the district lay amidst unusual and lovely scenery . . . I lived much out of doors and in companionship with Nature," and he had access to a good library.[14] His chief occupation was land surveying and map drawing. A short period thereafter was spent as secretary to the owner of estates in the Upper Palatinate, a province in the north of Bavaria, mainly concerned with accounting records.

While in this post, Froebel received news of his uncle's death and of a legacy to him. These events changed Froebel's life, marking the beginning of a period of self-discovery and of finding his true calling.

CHAPTER 2

Born Teacher

THE inheritance left to Froebel by his beloved uncle Hoffman was the means, as he put it, "of fulfilling the dearest wish of my life," namely "an eager desire for higher culture." At the time, architecture seemed to be an ideal profession for Froebel; so he went to Frankfurt in the summer of 1805, expecting to devote all his energies to architectural studies and to make this field his life work.

As he meditated on the future, however, Froebel started to feel doubts about his decision. He began to ask himself, in an idealistic frame of mind, "How can I work through architecture for the culture and ennobling of man?" Rationalizing the answer, he adhered to his original scheme and began study under an established architect. At that point there occurred a critical meeting. Froebel was introduced to Dr. Anton Gruener, headmaster of the Frankfurt Model School, a recently established institution that was being developed on Pestalozzian principles. Gruener strongly urged Froebel to abandon the idea of being an architect and instead to become a teacher in his school. Froebel quotes Gruener as saying, "My friend, you should not be an architect, you should be a schoolmaster. There is a place open in our school; if you agree to it the place is yours."[1]

Yielding to Gruener's persuasion, Froebel "accepted the summons as a call of Providence." Prior to beginning his new duties he decided to visit Pestalozzi at Yverdon to see and hear the great educational light of the day, the fountainhead of all new educational ideas. Froebel remained with Pestalozzi for two weeks, in August, 1805, attended recitations, and observed the school's operations. Returning to Frankfurt in October, he began to apply the ideas gleaned from his stay in Switzerland. The subjects assigned to Froebel were arithmetic, drawing, geometry, and the German

19

language. A class of thirty to forty boys, ranging in age from nine to eleven, met Froebel in his first teaching venture. The young teacher was then twenty-four years of age. His reactions to his new profession are vividly described in a letter to his brother Christoph:

I must tell you candidly that my duties in the school are prodigiously exacting. Even in the first hour they did not seem strange to me. It appeared to me as if I had already been a teacher and was born to it. I cannot sketch my strange observations in all their fullness. It is plain to me now that I was really fitted for no other calling, and yet I must tell you that never in my life had I thought to become a teacher. In the hours of instruction I feel myself as truly in my element as the fish in the water or the bird in the air. You cannot think how pleasantly the time passes. I love the children so heartily that I am continually longing to see them again. I have certainly this pure enjoyment of the consciousness of the high aims of my work, the cultivation of the human mind to think, as well as the hearty love of the children with which they reward me.[2]

Thus at last, after much uncertainty and floundering, Froebel discovered, more or less by chance, his true vocation. His short stay with Pestalozzi had an immediate effect on his teaching methods. For example, he followed the Pestalozzian principle of stressing firsthand knowledge, rather than empty theory, and of proceeding from the near to the remote. His lessons on physical geography were based on trips of discovery which he and his pupils made in the vicinity of Frankfurt—also one of Pestalozzi's favorite devices. Froebel admired most of the practices which he had observed in the Yverdon school, describing it as "a great educational institution." He approved especially of the so-called "exchange classes," a system under which the subjects for teaching were agreed upon for every class and pupils were distributed among the different classes according to their proficiency in the particular subject being taught. This scheme was adopted by Froebel in all his future teaching.

On the other hand, Froebel decided that the curriculum designed by Pestalozzi and his associates at Yverdon was incomplete and onesided. In his view, several important subjects were "treated in step-motherly fashion, and superficially worked out"—doubtless a reflection of Froebel's strong convictions on the interconnection and unity of all fields of study. The teaching of mathematics, despite its "brilliant results," was too mechanical; and the method used for the German language was "arbitrary and non-productive." Nevertheless, much of the teaching at Yverdon he found worthy of praise and emulation.

To his duties in the Frankfurt Model School, Froebel shortly added private tutoring. A Herr von Holzhausen and his wife were seeking a teacher for their three sons, and Froebel agreed to spend two hours daily giving them lessons in arithmetic and German and to share their walks. Pestalozzian principles were followed in arithmetic instruction, but serious difficulties were encountered in teaching German by the use of standard textbooks. Adoption of Pestalozzi's *Mothers' Book* methods proved more satisfactory, though Froebel states that "for a very long time no system of instruction in German did satisfy me."[3]

Indeed, Froebel found himself in opposition to virtually all existing teaching methods and felt a strong urge to reorganize the various subjects being taught into a connected whole. His thoughts on how to proceed in any practical fashion, however, remained hazy. Some clues were provided by observing and experimenting with his three private pupils. Herr von Holzhausen gave his sons a piece of meadowland for a garden. Froebel noted with satisfaction the delight which the boys experienced in their gardening operations and recognized that such activities could easily be turned to educational uses. When winter came, Froebel devised indoor amusements, such as modeling in paper, pasteboard, and wood. The enjoyment which his pupils evidently took in these exercises further convinced Froebel of the value of the creative instinct as a means of education. Walks with the children also provided opportunities for informal teaching, especially for natural history subjects. According to Froebel, he tried to the "utmost to penetrate into the lives of the children" in the course of which "I lived my own early life over again, but in a happier way."[4]

At this stage in his career, Froebel informs us, "All my thoughts and words were now directed to the subject of the culture and education of man. My life became full of zeal, of active development, of advancing culture, and, in consequence, of happiness. And my life in the Model School also, with my boys and with my excellent colleagues, unusually clever men, was very elevating and encouraging."[5]

In the Model School it was the custom, too, for the teachers to take their classes for walks in the surrounding countryside. Froebel utilized these periods to teach botany and geography. The varied physiographic features of the land—river, hills, distant mountains, and level stretches—made easier the drawing of graphic maps. At the next public examination of the school, Froebel's pupils demonstrated their accurate knowledge. "My boys were as well acquainted with the surroundings of the town as with their own rooms at home," Froebel states with pride, "and gave rapid and striking answers as to all the natural peculiarities of the neighborhood. This course was the fountainhead of the teaching method which I afterwards thoroughly worked out, and which has now been in use for many years."[6]

Always restless and still seeking better methods to improve his teaching, Froebel decided after a two-year stay to resign his position in the Model School at Frankfurt. The parents of the three boys to whom he had been giving private instruction persuaded him to become their full-time tutor. Froebel consented on condition that the children should be placed completely in his charge and live in isolation with him in the country, à la Rousseau's Émile. The experiment was not, however, altogether satisfactory; and Froebel soon realized that such a narrow and onesided life was undesirable for the boys and for himself. With the consent of the parents, therefore, in the summer of 1808 Froebel took his three pupils to Yverdon for a two-year sojourn with Pestalozzi. "So it soon afterwards came about," he remarks, "I was teacher and scholar, educator and pupil, all at the same time."[7] Idealistically, Froebel writes that he "expected to find at Yverdon a vigorous inner life amongst the boys and youths, quickening, manifesting itself in all kinds of creative activity, satisfying the manysidedness of man, meeting all his necessities, and occupying all his powers both mental and bodily."[8] The realities, of course, were bound to fall somewhat short of these high hopes.

At the time of Froebel's return visit, Pestalozzi's institute had about two hundred pupils of different nationalities. Though space was not available in the main building, Froebel found lodging for himself and his three charges in the immediate proximity so that they "were able to join the pupils at their dinner, their evening meal, and their supper, and to take part in the whole courses of their instruction, so far as the subjects chosen by us were concerned; indeed to share in their whole life."[9] Again, and even more strongly than before, Froebel felt the inspiration of Pestalozzi's presence, declaring: "He set one's soul on fire for a higher and nobler life, though he had not made clear or sure the exact road towards it nor indicated the means whereby to attain it."[10]

As Froebel remarks, he "soon saw much that was imperfect" in the Yverdon institution. He felt keenly the lack of unity in the work as a whole and in many of its departments and the absence of clear insight into the nature of the means and methods employed. Still the stay at Yverdon was of immense value to him and he spoke afterwards of his two years there as "a glorious time." He gained much from the training in physiography and nature study that he gave his pupils during long walks in the country; he found opportunities to study the play of children in its effects upon both intellectual and physical development; he first came to see the importance of early training of a child by its mother; and his knowledge of music, which was later such a basic part of his methods, was greatly enlarged. In a negative way, the lack of organization and deficiency in unity and interconnection of studies, always evident in Pestalozzi's work, convinced Froebel that he should eliminate vagueness in aim and method by making specific the underlying principles in the teaching of various subjects. His thinking on these matters was clarified by discussions with Pestalozzi concerning the relationship of each branch of instruction to others and possible means to achieve the best results. Similar talks were held with the institute's teachers and with the children themselves. To further his own understanding of and insight into the unity of all knowledge, Froebel made a conscious effort to gain a working facility in all subjects—arithmetic, form, singing, reading, drawing, language, physical geography, the natural sciences, etc.

Commenting on specific subjects as taught at Yverdon, Froebel notes that "the teaching of languages struck me with especial force as defective, on account of its great imperfection, its capriciousness and lifelessness." The search for a satisfactory method to teach native languages became Froebel's first priority. On the other hand, the teaching of music and singing in the institute he found was excellent, with two instructors, Nägeli and Pfeifer, highly qualified in the field. Twenty years later, Froebel recalled that "the fire of the love for music which they kindled burns yet, active for good, within my breast."[11]

At the end of the two-year period, having decided that he had gained as much benefit as possible from the stay with Pestalozzi at Yverdon, Froebel returned in 1810 with his pupils to Frankfurt. The following year, having fulfilled his contract with the von Holzhausen family, he entered the University of Göttingen, determined to continue preparation for the educational career to which his life was henceforth to be devoted. His mother's sister had just died, leaving him enough money to make his university stay financially secure for a short time.

Froebel felt that his greatest deficiency was in languages and he therefore entered into an ambitious program of linguistic studies. He was especially attracted by Oriental languages and immersed himself in the study of Persian, Hebrew, Arabic, and also Greek. The lack of proper textbooks continually frustrated and discouraged him, however, as it had done earlier. He noted that "between the manner of looking at a language congenial to my mind and the manner in which the elementary lesson book presented it to me, lay a vast chasm which I could find no means to bridge over."[12] Froebel's desire to study languages as living organisms was simply not feasible with the tools available. In the end he abandoned everything except Greek, which he found "irresistibly enthralling"; and thereafter he stated that "nearly all my time and energy were finally given to its study, with the help of the best books." His visionary idea at the outset had been to discover that all of the world's languages were descended from a common source and to create a true linguistic science by cutting through the diversity of human speech and the confusion of tongues. Froebel's constant preoccupation with the concept of the unity of all things in nature, including the unity of speech, again emerges here.

While at Göttingen, Froebel continued also his scientific studies—physics, chemistry, mineralogy, and natural science—a field for which he had greater aptitude than for languages. Later in the one year spent at the University of Göttingen, he concentrated on organic chemistry and geology. Time was even found to attend lectures in history, political science, and economics. Froebel found unconvincing and unacceptable the views on fixed forms in the teaching of crystallography, mineralogy, and science in general at Göttingen. The lectures of Professor Weiss on natural history and mineralogy at the University of Berlin were attracting much attention at the time. Froebel, certain that he could acquire a "correct view" from Weiss, left Göttingen and entered the recently established university at Berlin in October, 1812.

The Weiss lectures quite lived up to Froebel's expectations. As a contemporary critic, Wichard Lange, commented, they strengthened his belief "that all life, that is, development into a whole, was founded upon one law, and that this unity must be the basis of all principles of development, its beginning and end. This conviction was the result of a profound study of nature in its law of development, and the most careful contemplation of the child."[13]

The point should be emphasized that all of Froebel's continued studies and work at this stage in his career were directed toward improving his understanding of the science and means of education. While at Berlin he never lost sight of his primary concern for child study, and in fact he was earning a living in large measure by teaching in the Pestalozzian school for boys being conducted there by Johann Ernst Plamann.

In the course of Froebel's Berlin studies, the city was in a turmoil of revolt against Napoleon's domination of Germany. The patriotic Froebel, now aged thirty-one, heeded the King's call to arms and enlisted in the infantry division of the "Lutzow Jagers," at Dresden. The corps became celebrated for swift, dashing exploits in small bodies, designed to harass the enemy by constant skirmishes, a kind of guerilla warfare, though there is little evidence that Froebel's regiment engaged in any extensive combat operations. Peace came in May, 1814.

The military regime never took Froebel's mind off the subject of education. "Everywhere," he wrote, "as far as the fatigues I underwent allowed, I carried in my thoughts my future calling as educator; yes, even in the few engagements in which I had to take part. Even in these I could gather experience for the task I proposed to myself." The military life showed Froebel the value of discipline and cooperative action.[14]

From the point of view of his future career the most important consequence of Froebel's military service was friendships formed with two younger comrades, Wilhelm Middendorff and Heinrich Langethal. Middendorff and Langethal had been divinity students at Berlin prior to joining the army. Both men became Froebel's lifelong friends and disciples, and in the history of kindergarten education their names are closely linked with his own.

When Froebel began his military service, he received the promise of a position under the Prussian government at the end of the war. In July, 1814, accordingly, he was back in Berlin to accept an appointment as assistant to Professor Weiss in the Royal Museum of Mineralogy. The post provided him with an opportunity not only to continue his mineralogical studies but also to attend university lectures and to develop his educational plans. "While engaged in this work," Froebel recalled, "It continually proved to be true what had long been a presentiment with me that even in these so-called lifeless stones and fragments of rock, torn from their original bed, there lay germs of transforming, developing energy and activity. Among the diversity of forms around me, I recognized under all kinds of various modifications one law of development. Therefore my rocks and crystals served me as a mirror wherein I might descry mankind and man's development and history."[15]

In striking contrast to the military life, during which he had been thrown in close daily association with a large body of men engaged in a common cause, Froebel's museum duties were largely isolated from people. Fascinated as he was, however, by his crystals, Froebel's dominating interest always was in humanity. Partly under the stimulus of a series of lectures on ancient philosophy which he attended and partly because of talks on educational matters which he had with his friends Middendorff and Langethal, both of whom were serving as private tutors, Froebel's thoughts turned increasingly to problems of language and education.

The better system of education now visualized by Froebel would combine the improvements introduced by Pestalozzi with a unity which the latter's system lacked. The urgent need of the time, Froebel was convinced, was "a more human, related, affiliated, connected treatment and consideration of the subjects of education."[16] In the belief that he could supply the missing element, Froebel declined a professorship of mineralogy in Stockholm and resigned his position in Berlin in October, 1816. Thenceforth, for the remaining thirty-six years of his life, Friedrich Froebel's time, energy, and thought were wholly devoted to the world of education.

CHAPTER 3

Always the Educator

FROEBEL resumed his active teaching career at the age of thirty-four. Everything in which he had been engaged up to this point contributed to his preparation for the educational profession: the practical experience in Gruener's school; the period of observation, learning, and teaching at Yverdon; tutoring the three von Holzhausen sons; the university years at Jena, Göttingen, and Berlin; the discipline of a soldier's life; and the insights into science provided by work in the mineralogical museum at Berlin. He had also thought deeply about the aims and nature of education.

The immediate reason for Froebel's decision to resign his position in the mineralogical museum in Berlin was a family crisis. Christoph Froebel, his favorite older brother, who had so frequently come to his aid in the past, died of typhus fever in 1813, while nursing French soldiers in hospitals. Christoph left a wife and three children. The widow wrote to Friedrich expressing her anxiety regarding the proper education of the boys and appealing to him for advice. It was this communication which caused Froebel to make up his mind to return to teaching and, as a first step, to assume responsibility for the education of his nephews. On his way from Berlin, he stopped at Osterode, where his brother Christian had become a spinner and dyer of linen thread. The brothers agreed that Friedrich should open a school at Griesheim, the widow's residence, the pupils to include the three sons of Christoph and Christian's two sons. Friedrich began his teaching on November 16, 1816, calling his new school the "Universal German Educational Institute"—a rather grandiloquent title for a teacher with five pupils housed in a peasant's cottage.

The school remained at Griesheim only a few months. In the summer of 1817 Froebel's sister-in-law decided to move her family

27

to Keilhau, ten miles away, where she bought a small farm. The
school went with her and was reopened June 24, 1817. The hamlet
of Keilhau, where Froebel was destined to establish much of his
fame as an educator, is on a mountainside in the Thuringian Forest,
some five miles southwest of Rudolstadt, a region of great natural
beauty.

The primitive state of the village of Keilhau as late as 1815 was
described by a contemporary writer: "Although not poor, the
peasants had remained in the condition of the Middle Ages.
. . . The church with its pretty tower was nevertheless more like a
cellar than the house of God. In the midst of the village a water
course marked the street and five springs kept the road wet all the
time. There were only about one hundred inhabitants and the living
of the peasants was very simple."[1]

Before the opening of the school at Griesheim, Froebel had
written to Wilhelm Middendorff at Berlin inviting him and
Heinrich Langethal to join him in helping to work out a new system
of education. In April, 1817, Middendorff came and Langethal
followed in September. At Keilhau, Froebel and Middendorff for
some time occupied a wretched little hut with no door, flooring, or
stove. By November, however, a frame house had been set up in the
farmyard.

An important event in Froebel's life during this period was his
marriage in September, 1818, to Henrietta Willhelmine Hoffmeister, whom he had met in the Berlin museum. Froebel describes
her as "a lady with a like love of nature and of childhood as my
own, and a like high and earnest conception of education."[2] Frau
Froebel appears to have been an admirable, self-sacrificing, and
highly cultured woman who shared her husband's complete dedication to education and was willing to endure the hardships and
privations that marked most of their years together until her death
in 1839.

When Froebel first came to Griesheim, he had told Christoph's
widow that he wished to be a father to her orphaned children—an
ambiguous statement which she had interpreted as an intention to
marry her. There are two accounts of what happened as a result of
this emotional, well-intentioned remark. According to one, when
Froebel's sister-in-law learned that he planned to wed Fraulein
Hoffmeister, she angrily demanded that her ungrateful brother-in-
law return the money she had invested in the school and threatened

to sell the Keilhau property, to take the boys out of the school, and to go to the magistrate for her rights. A conflicting report states that when Christoph's widow learned of Friedrich's engagement, she deeded her property to him and in June, 1818 went to Valkstadt to live. Whether Froebel committed himself to pay for the property is a moot point.

In any event, the school at Keilhau was facing financial disaster within two years. Froebel writes concerning the privations of that period: "We had now a severe struggle for existence for the whole time up to 1820. With all our efforts we never could get the schoolhouse enlarged; other still more necessary buildings had to be erected first."[3] As an example of the straits to which Froebel was reduced, an associate mentioned that in the school's early days he lived for a week on two loaves of bread.

Fortunately, the businessman of the Froebel brothers, Christian, decided to move his family to Keilhau and join Friedrich's venture. Christian invested his whole fortune in the institute, thereby meeting the most pressing obligations. About the same time, Middendorff's father died, and the son immediately turned over his inheritance to the school. During the next six years the number of pupils grew from twenty to sixty. New buildings were erected and several more teachers were appointed. In 1823, Johannes Arnold Barop, Middendorff's nephew, a divinity student at Halle, visited Keilhau and decided to remain as a teacher. Eventually, he became the mainstay of the whole enterprise.

But given Friedrich Froebel's notable lack of managerial ability and want of financial sense, the school's problems steadily accumulated. Concerning this period, Barop wrote:

About 1827 we were in an unusually critical position. You know how little means we had when we began to create our institution. Middendorff had sacrificed his entire inheritance from his father, but the purchase of the ground and the erection of necessary buildings called for considerable sums, so that Middendorff's addition to the capital had disappeared like drops of water falling on a hot stove. My father-in-law, Christian Ludwig Froebel, had later on come forward and placed his entire fortune unconditionally in the hands of his brother, but even this sacrifice was not sufficient to keep away care and want from the door.[4]

Froebel's and the school's difficulties were compounded by community hostilities, also described by Barop: "Mistrust surrounded us on all sides in those early years of our work; open and concealed enmities assailed us both from near and far, and sought to embitter our lot and to nip our efforts in the bud."[5] The number of pupils sank to five or six, cash receipts dwindled while debts grew and creditors became more persistent.

For a brief time it appeared that the Duke of Meiningen would come to the rescue of the school by providing financial aid; but when the duke was persuaded by his most influential adviser on educational matters that the Keilhau enterprise was unsound, he withdrew an anticipated subsidy. Like Heinrich Pestalozzi and Horace Mann, two other great educational pioneers, Froebel was highly impractical in material matters. His philanthropic nature made it impossible for him to turn away an orphan or a widow's child. Thus, even when the Keilhau school had its largest enrollment, student fees were insufficient to maintain the institution. Froebel himself was too completely engrossed in putting into effect his cherished views on education to give thought to economic considerations.

Local opposition to the Keilhau school derived in part from unorthodox behavior on the part of its staff and pupils, who had adopted the German dress and had allowed their hair to grow long. The Prussian government became suspicious of the school, and in September, 1824 the Prince of Schwarzburg-Rudolstadt appointed a Superintendent Zeb to inspect and to report upon Keilhau and its activities.

Zeb paid two visits to the school in November, 1824 and March, 1825, and then submitted a highly favorable report, stating, in part:

I found here what is never and nowhere shown in real life, a timely and closely united family of some sixty members, living in quiet harmony, all showing that they gladly perform the duties of their various positions; a family in which, because it is held together by the strong hand of mutual confidence, and because every member seeks the good of the whole, everything, as of itself, thrives in happiness and love.[6]

Zeb noted that as principal Froebel was held in respect and affection; "the little five-year-old children clung to his knees," and his colleagues relied upon his insights, experience, and advice. "Self activity of mind," Zeb commented, "is the first law of the institution; . . . slowly, continuously, gradually and always inwardly, that is ac-

cording to a connection founded upon the nature of the human
mind, the instruction steadily goes on, without any tricks, from the
simple to the complex, from the concrete to the abstract, so well-
adapted to the child and his needs that he goes as readily to his
learning as to his play."[7] On the basis of such a laudatory report, the
prince could not justify proceeding with the original intention of
closing the institute, but simply directed the Keilhau group to cut
their hair and dress like the people of the community at large.

The agitation which led to Zeb's investigation, however, caused
nearly all the patrons of the school to withdraw their children from
it. One of the teachers, a Swiss, Karl Herzog, organized opposition
to Froebel and after he left the school spread libelous stories about
the institute for some time afterward. Under Herzog's influence,
Froebel's sister-in-law also broke with the school and took her three
sons with her. By 1829, Keilhau had only five pupils enrolled.

A revealing glimpse of Keilhau in its most prosperous days, prior
to the advent of these various misfortunes, comes from the
reminiscences of Colonel Hermann von Arnswald, who was a pupil
in the school for three years, 1824 - 1826. According to Arnswald's
account, when he arrived at the school, Froebel took him immediately to meet the other boys; and he soon felt completely at
home. Strict order was observed in the domestic life of the institution, and personal cleanliness was required. Pupils went through inspection each morning before breakfast, and those deficient in
neatness received only bread and no milk. Any boy responsible for
property damage at Keilhau was required personally to make
repairs. Von Arnswald reported that during his three years at the
school, no physician ever entered the institution. Small injuries
were treated by the boys themselves. There were no vacation
periods, but a tramp through the woods, sometimes extended for
days, was a frequent feature of the summer session. The anniversary
of the battle of Leipzig, which forced Napoleon's armies to
withdraw from Germany, was celebrated by a mountain-top fire in
the evening, at which time, Arnswald recalled, "popular and
patriotic songs were sung, and we listened to the inspiring words of
our teachers, every one of whom had fought through the wars of
deliverance as a volunteer, all having been faithful comrades in the
service of the great fatherland."[8] When winter came, there were
frequent sleigh rides on the ice.

Von Arnswald concludes his story by observing: "I lived at

Keilhau for three years. At the end of that time I went home to the house of my parents healthy in soul and body. After a life so natural and so completely secluded from all the injurious impressions of the outside world there could not have been any other result than perfect health."[9]

Another pupil at Keilhau, George Ebers, gives further insight into the school's activities:

We took long walks up the mountains or in the forest, the older pupils acting as teachers. We discovered every variety of insect on the bushes and in the moss, the turf, the bark of trees, on the flowers and blades of grass. We listened to the note of birds; and how many trees we climbed, what steep cliffs we also climbed, through what crevices we squeezed, to add a rare egg to our collection. Our teachers' love for all animate creation had made them impose bounds on our zeal, so we were required always to leave one egg in the nest, and if it contained but one not to molest it.[10]

Again, according to Ebers' account, "every boy was to be educated according to his peculiar temperament, with special regard to his disposition, talents, and character." A record of achievement was maintained for each individual and a copy sent to parents "containing a description of character, a criticism of the work accomplished, partly with reference to the pupil's capacity, partly to the demand of the school." Ebers commented that "some of these records are little masterpieces of psychological penetration."[11] A system of student government was established. Penalties for misbehavior, ranging from outright expulsion for grave offenses to confinement to house or courtyard for minor misdemeanors, were fixed by the pupils themselves.

A fundamental idea with Froebel, at Keilhau and later, was that a child should not be treated as only receptive, but also, and especially, as a creative, productive being. He sought constantly to arouse the child's curiosity, to persuade him to ask questions, and to seek explanations. Manual work was regarded as a prime means of achieving these objectives.

Froebel was head of the Keilhau school for fourteen years. The highest number of pupils enrolled during that period was about sixty. As an educational experiment the institution was an undoubted success, despite constant financial troubles. Apparently, no one associated with the school realized the considerable sums of money required to operate such an organization without state support.

Two important developments destined to shape Froebel's future occurred near the end of his tenure as principal of the Keilhau school. Mainly through correspondence, Froebel had become acquainted with the well-known philosopher Karl Krause; and in the fall of 1828 Froebel and Middendorff traveled to Göttingen to visit Krause and to discuss topics of mutual interest. Long talks on education took place during this celebrated meeting. Krause was thoroughly familiar with the writings of Comenius (1592 - 1670) and drew Froebel's attention to the wise old Czech bishop's treatise on the earliest education of children, *Schola Materni Gremii*. It is probable that this discussion helped to turn Froebel's mind to the field in which he would achieve his greatest success, the kindergarten.

The second event to cause a major change in Froebel's life occurred on a visit in 1831 to Frankfurt, where he had gone to see his many friends, among them Gruener, who had started him on his educational career, and Frau von Holzhausen, who had from the first understood and sympathized with his aspirations and ideas. While in Frankfurt, Froebel met the musician and composer Xavier Schnyder of Wartensee, Switzerland, a person of culture and an experienced teacher and educator, whose background enabled him to appreciate fully Froebel's scheme of education. Schnyder had worked with Pestalozzi and was a friend of Hans Georg Naegeli, eminent Swiss composer and a member of the Yverdon faculty. Schnyder studied carefully the plan prepared by Froebel and his Keilhau associates. So impressed was he with the value, importance, and originality of the work that he offered to put at Froebel's disposal the Castle of Wartensee on the Lake of Sempach in Switzerland, for an educational institution. The generous offer was accepted by Froebel with delight.

The move to Switzerland led to Froebel's practical relinquishment of control of the Keilhau institution, though he would spend many months there in later years.

CHAPTER 4

Swiss Interlude

IMMEDIATELY following Xavier Schnyder's offer to make his castle at Wartensee available for a new type of educational institution, Froebel started for Switzerland, accompanied by his nephew Ferdinand and Schnyder himself. On August 12, 1831, the necessary authorization was obtained from the Swiss Minister of Education to start a Froebel school in the Canton of Lucerne. The permit, in the form of a letter addressed to Schnyder, read:

We have the pleasure of sending you and Herrn Friedrich Froebel the decision of the Council which met on the 10th inst., and which authorizes you to establish in the Canton a private model school such as you have described. We congratulate the Canton on the prospect of having a school under such excellent management, and one which is likely to have so good an influence on the other schools of the Canton. We shall have the honor to interest ourselves especially in this institution, and at all times be ready to do anything in our power to further so beneficent an undertaking.[1]

A circular dated August 3, 1831, announced the opening of "The Wartensee Institution," to receive German, French, and Italian children of the surrounding cantons. German was to be the primary language of instruction. The pupils were to be prepared for commerce, trade, or the university. The castle, so magnanimously put at Froebel's disposal by Schnyder, with its furniture, silver, and excellent library, appeared at first an ideal setting. It was beautifully located in view of the Bernese Oberland, and looking in different directions toward Germany, France, and Italy. Froebel's desire to continue Pestalozzi's work in the great reformer's own country seemed near realization.

But controversy followed Froebel to Switzerland. Shortly after the announcement of the opening of the new school there appeared

34

an anonymous newspaper article, entitled "A Word about Friedrich Froebel of Keilhau, Founder of the Wartensee Institution," making baseless charges against Froebel and Schnyder. A refutation of the charges, intended to vindicate Froebel and his system, was drawn up and sent to the Council of Education at Lucerne. A few months later, a second attack appeared, written by Froebel's long-time enemy, Karl Herzog, who had been discharged from the Keilhau faculty for creating dissension. By this time, however, Froebel had gained staunch Swiss friends, who wrote several articles in the *Argau News* attesting to the excellence of the school and the ability and integrity of its founders.

A typical school day at Wartensee is described in Froebel's own words:

I am so busy up to three o'clock, that there is hardly time for breakfast or lunch, and I often work on till late in the night. Lessons begin punctually at eight, although many of the pupils have to come long distances and sometimes through the fiercest weather. After prayers the first lesson is arithmetic, Ferdinand taking one division, I the other; we also share the language teaching that follows. From ten to eleven my nephew gives the upper division a lesson on the history of Switzerland, and the little ones read with me or draw in chequers. . . . The feeling for art is like a magnet. It soothes the children and keeps them at the table till I break up the class by main force. . . . By a few minutes past one everything is in order, and we are all quietly at work again. The older children do their French exercises, while the little ones draw. At two o'clock the little ones write German with me, and the big ones have an oral French lesson. School is over at three. On fine days we have games and gymnastics in the grounds, after which the children disperse.[2]

Froebel's associates back at Keilhau were concerned about his new venture and sent Barop to Wartensee to investigate and report on progress. Before he reached his destination, Barop stopped in the neighborhood to make inquiries about the institution, and was informed that the teachers were a company of heretics. The opposition of the local clergy against the "heretics" and foreigners was from the first virulent and aggressive. The result was that children residing at considerable distances and those from well-to-do families did not come, a fact which drastically affected the school's income. Clerical criticism also caused people of the community to be continually suspicious of Froebel's motives in establishing the school. Barop writes, "The ill-will of the clergy, which began to show itself immediately the institution was founded, and which became stronger as the footing of our friends grew firmer, was able to gather to itself a following sufficient to check any quick growth of our undertaking."[3] Barop began to doubt that even here, in the land of freedom, Froebel had found the right home for his efforts.

A further complication was the unsuitability of Schnyder's castle for the school. Schnyder would permit no new buldings or alterations of any kind, and Barop states that "the rooms assigned to us were in no way suitable for our use."

The way out of the dilemma was found by chance, during an incident which was to give the school a fresh start. Froebel, Middendorff, and Barop had gone for a walk and had stopped at a neighborhood restaurant for refreshments. As they sat discussing the school and its work, some merchants from Willisau, a nearby town, overheard their conversation and joined in. The merchants showed a keen interest in the aims and objects of the new school, and on their return to Willisau sent an inviation to Froebel to come there and establish a similar institution. About twenty well-to-do families guaranteed the necessary funds and agreed to provide some old government offices to serve as schoolrooms. The necessary authorization for the opening of the school was received in April, 1833, and in May Froebel and his wife met Barop and Ferdinand Froebel in Willisau. The school opened with thirty-six pupils. Barop comments, "Now we seemed at last to have found what we had so long been seeking." The larger population of Willisau made the location more suitable for carrying out Froebel's educational scheme.

But again clerical opposition erupted. As Barop writes, "The priests rose up furiously against us with a really devilish force. We even went in fear of our lives, and were often warned by kind-hearted people to turn back, when we were walking toward secluded spots, or had struck along the outlying paths amongst the mountains."[4] Froebel's and his associates' chief crime was that they were Protestants, a fact sufficient to create alarm in the prevailing Catholic mind. The better-educated classes approved of the school and patronized it. On the other side, the clergy stirred up the peasants to such an extent that there was virtually a religious panic.

Petitions, appeals, and attacks, many with crosses for signatures, began to pour in from all sections of the canton. In the midst of the crisis, Barop, serving as the school's ambassador, applied to the municipality for protection. The magistrate, Edward Pfyffer, a man of intelligence and education, offered sage advice: "There is only one way: that is to win over the people; stick to your work for a little while, and then invite people from far and near to a public demonstration. If this succeeds you are protected, not otherwise."[5]

The magistrate's counsel was accepted and the demonstration was arranged on a beautiful autumn day in 1833. Crowds flocked to Willisau from all the neighboring cantons, among them government officials from Berne, Zurich, and other towns, drawn by newspaper stories and the prolonged controversy. The examination lasted the entire day, ending with games and gymnastics. A complete victory was won, with the eagerness and simplicity of the children charming the audience. A public conference followed, participated in by the school's friends and educational authorities. A resolution was passed to grant Froebel the building used for the school at a moderate rental and to banish the priests who incited crowds to riot from the canton.

The religious persecution suffered by Froebel at Wartensee and Willisau was similar to Heinrich Pestalozzi's experience thirty-five years earlier in his school for poor children and orphans at Stans, and for the same reasons.

The Willisau school had other obstacles to overcome besides the opposition of the Catholic clergy. Concerning these problems, Froebel writes: "It seems to me that education in the canton is more hindered by selfishness and egotism even than by bigotry. The public approves of the education proposed for them, the means are ready to hand, but no one will take the first step. Our public demonstrations have awakened in the minds of the public a desire for the new education; but they act like people who, though they want their cow to give good milk, are unwilling to provide it with good food and shelter."[6]

The Bernese government showed its confidence in Froebel by sending some young teachers to Willisau to be trained. A delegation also came from Berne to invite Froebel to undertake the organization of an orphanage at Burgdorf. The invitation was accepted; and in the summer of 1835 Froebel, Langethal, and their wives settled in Burgdorf, leaving Middendorff in charge of the Willisau establishment. Several activities were carried on concurrently by Froebel at Burgdorf. There was a day school for the children of the town, and a boarding school was started for pupils living at a distance. In addition, there was a training class of sixty students preparing to be teachers. The Bernese government had arranged that every teacher in the canton should have three months leave of absence in the year to enable them to attend Froebel's classes and conferences. Such a diverse program naturally plunged Froebel into manifold difficulties and problems associated with elementary education.

Despite a heavy work load, Froebel and his wife spent a happy time at Burgdorf, surrounded as they were by spectacular Alpine scenery. Besides being the head of two thriving institutions—Keilhau, now under Barop's direction, and Willisau, where Middendorff was carrying on—Froebel held an influential position in the most advanced canton of Switzerland. Teachers and pupils were devoted to him; and his present site, Burgdorf, was closely associated with Pestalozzi. Evidently, however, Froebel was never content with the status quo; he was always in an intellectual ferment, seeking ways and means to put into practice the idea which had long occupied his mind: "the complete development of the child from within outwards." To achieve this goal, Froebel felt that it was essential to begin with the earliest years of a child's life. Accordingly, he organized a department for children from age three, who would then proceed, somewhere between four and six, into the lowest class of the elementary school. His own observations and work with teachers at Burgdorf had convinced Froebel that all school education was as yet without proper foundation. That basis must be laid with reform of education in the nursery.

Concerning this period in Froebel's life, Barop writes: "The necessity of training gifted, capable mothers occupied his soul, and the importance of the education of childhood's earliest years became more evident to him than ever. He determined to set forth fully his ideas on education, which the tyranny of a thousand opposing circumstances had always prevented him from working out in their completeness; or at all events to do this as regards the earliest years of man, and then to win over the world of women to the actual accomplishment of his plans."[7]

At Burgdorf, Froebel had noted the young child's early observations of his surroundings, and his eagerness to express his understanding of them. To aid the child in expressing himself, Froebel would provide him with rhymes, songs and games, objects and materials for manipulation, gymnastic exercises, and simple stories and poems. In a study of children at play, Froebel noted that play to the youngest child "is the great game of life itself in its beginnings. Hence the intense seriousness often observed in the attitude of children at play."[8] The logical starting point for infant education was a reform of family life, and especially the training of the mother. The home, like the school, Froebel concluded, must be adapted to the child's development. Mother and teacher must work toward the same end. The primary goal envisioned by Froebel was a system of education that would be steadily progressive from first to last, an end which required the training of mothers to stimulate the child's powers in such a manner that he would grow and flourish "as a plant does under favorable conditions." Here was the problem, the solution of which led Froebel directly to the creation of the kindergarten.

After a three-year stay at Burgdorf, Frau Froebel's health broke down and, seeking a milder climate, she and her husband returned to Germany. By this time, 1836, the idea of an institution for the education of little children had fully taken shape in Froebel's mind. He naturally felt that his native Germany was the proper place to develop these plans, and he never returned to Switzerland.

At the time of Froebel's departure, the Willisau institution was apparently flourishing; its activities were increasingly limited, however, by the bigotry of the priests. It was soon to be given up, since the government had passed into the hands of the Jesuit party. Froebel's work there was continued until 1839 by Middendorff and Ferdinand Froebel. Langethal and Ferdinand Froebel became directors of the Burgdorf school. Later, Langethal resigned to become head of a girl's school in Berne. Ferdinand continued the work until his sudden death a few years later. Middendorff meanwhile returned to Keilhau.

Thus the educational experiments in Switzerland, so far as Froebel was concerned, lasted for a relatively brief period of time and achieved only limited success, considering the mental and physical effort expended upon them. But Froebel was now primed to proceed with his innovative contributions to the kindergarten field.

CHAPTER 5

Origins of the Kindergarten

THE practice of assembling circles of small children for educational purposes has ancient antecedents. Children's circles were known to the Greeks in the time of Plato and Aristotle. A more modern infant school was that of Pastor Oberlin, at Walbach, Alsace, in the late eighteenth century. The weavers' infant school, established at New Lanark, Scotland, in 1816, for "songs, games, and discipline," and supported by the philanthropist Robert Owen, was patterned after the Oberlin school.

Owen's *Autobiography* dwells at some length on his views of infant education. Owen, wealthy manufacturer and social reformer, too, was convinced of the imperative necessity of beginning with children in their earliest years; for, he stated, "to a great extent the character is made or marred before children enter the usual schoolroom." The Infant School at New Lanark accepted all children above one year of age. The teachers—James Buchanan, a simple-hearted weaver, and Molly Young, a girl of seventeen—were instructed by Owen to have unlimited patience with the children and to refrain from using harsh words or actions. Rather than teaching from books, the pupils "were to be taught the uses and nature of the common things around them, by familiar conversation when the children's curiosity was excited so as to induce them to ask questions respecting them."[1] The schoolroom was furnished with paintings, chiefly of animals, with maps, and often with natural objects from gardens, fields, and woods. Owen reports that small children following this scheme of education made remarkable progress; they "were unlike all children of such situated parents, and indeed unlike the children of any class in society."[2]

There were other forerunners of Froebel. Lord Brougham's infant schools, scattered throughout England, were supported by the Marquis of Lansdowne, the Duke of Devonshire, Wilberforce

Macaulay (father of the historian), and others. Crèches, for the daytime care of infants of working parents, were established in various places in Germany from 1802 to 1835. Though these institutions left much to be desired, they did serve to draw attention to the need for educating infants. Infant schools and crèches were primarily set up for the benefit of the poor and were aimed at relieving the mother of the burden of child care rather than at developing the child. Crèches were generally placed under the care of women who were ignorant of any method adapted to the child's educational needs and who were unable to earn their living in any other way.

Certain educational philosophers also influenced Froebel. Foremost among these were Comenius, Rousseau, and Pestalozzi, in whose writings are to be found the germinal ideas of the kindergarten. Comenius, born late in the sixteenth century—a student of education, a teacher, minister, and supervisor of schools—, wrote several valuable textbooks concerning childhood education. His *Orbis Pictus,* the first illustrated textbook for children, and *School of the Mothers' Knee* clearly foreshadow the kindergarten. The latter work points out to mothers how they can begin the education of their children at an early age.

About a century later, Rousseau produced his *Emile,* a treatise on education according to nature which held that the child's education should come from the free development of his own nature, his own powers, his own natural inclinations. Rousseau condemns the customary restrictions of swaddling clothes and other restraints on freedom of the body and advocates a maximum of outdoor life. In his words, "Nature desires that children should be children before they are men."

The impact of Pestalozzian principles on Froebel's views of education has been previously discussed. Pestalozzi draws an analogy between a child's development and that of the natural growth of a plant or animal:

Sound education stands before me symbolized by a tree planted near fertilizing waters. A little seed which contains the design of the tree—its form and properties—is placed in the soil. The whole tree is an uninterrupted chain of organic parts, the plan of which existed in the seed and root. Man is similar to the tree. In the new born child are hidden those faculties which are to unfold during life. It is not the educator who puts new powers and faculties into man—he only takes care that no untoward influence shall disturb nature's march of development.[3]

Froebel also saw the child as a growing organism, developing through creative activity. Space and time are allowed young plants and animals, he writes, "because we know that in accordance with laws that live in them they will develop properly and grow well; arbitrary interference with their growth is avoided." On the other hand, often misguidedly, "the young human being is looked upon as a piece of wax, a lump of clay, which man can mould as he pleases."[4]

When Froebel returned from Switzerland, the concept of a school for infants was fully formulated in his mind. At first, however, he was undecided on a suitable name for such an institution. The term "kindergarten" came to him by inspiration one day during a walk with Barop and Middendorff. Earlier suggestions to adopt the term "infant school" or "nursery school for little children" were rejected because the kindergarten was not to be a school in the traditional sense; the children were not to be schooled but freely developed. As described by Froebel, it was to be a "general institution for the complete culture of child-life up to school-age." In a striking comparison, Froebel explains, "As in a garden, under God's favor, and by the care of a skilled, intelligent gardener, growing plants are cultivated in accordance with Nature's laws, so here, in our child-garden, our kindergarten, shall the noblest of all growing things, men (that is children, the germs and shoots of humanity) be cultivated in accordance with the laws of their own being, of God and of Nature."[5]

Froebel decided to establish his first kindergarten at Blankenburg, a village near Keilhau, in the Thuringian Forest. Here he opened in 1837 what he called "a school for the psychological training of little children by means of play and occupations."[6] In order to provide operating funds, an appeal was broadcast to German women and girls. The plan included the founding of a model school, in which little children would learn through use of educational games and occupations devised by Froebel, and an allied institution for the training of teachers to undertake the earliest care and education of childhood.

The object of the kindergarten, in Froebel's words, is "to take the oversight of children before they are ready for school life, to exert an influence over their whole being in correspondence with its nature; to strengthen their bodily powers; to employ the awakening mind; to make them thoughtfully acquainted with the world of nature and of man; to guide heart and soul in a right direction, and lead them to the origin of all life, and to union with him."[7] Children's keen desire for incessant activity in movement, in thought, and in creative action was to be cherished and encouraged.

Froebel saw the family as the child's first school. In the atmosphere of family love he follows his self-active instincts. The kindergarten then becomes an extended family, in which the child learns consciously to use senses and limbs and to develop in harmony with his nature, while it supplies knowledge and means usually beyond the reach of home training. The impact of his own experiences is reflected in Froebel's belief that children frequently lack security and love in the home and that education should start as soon as possible in order to develop warmth and understanding between parents and children. Family unity, Froebel insisted, is the most important factor in education. A prime virtue for the mother is gentleness, in the father wise guidance. A home united by love is the best institution for human progress. When the home fails in its responsibilities, it is the educator's duty to instruct the parents along the right paths.

In the Blankenburg Kindergarten and apparently in others started by Froebel, a considerable part of the children's time was spent on gardening; for Froebel believed that each child should have a small garden of his own and that there should be two large beds common to all, one for flowers and one for vegetables. Froebel's hope was that the child would want to tend his own garden for his own enjoyment; even more fundamentally, it was expected that the child would realize he was one part of a larger garden and that he was responsible for keeping his own section well cultivated. A child in looking after his own plants would see the development of each one and perhaps recognize that he too was growing up.

A typical Froebel kindergarten is described in a small book, *Die Kindergarten*, by Middendorff:

When all have arrived, the children form a circle, moving lightly and happily, singing a cheerful song. . . . Then they take their seats at a long table and look around for some means of playing out the ideas which are filling their minds more or less clearly. At their request, small boxes of blocks are given them and they begin without delay to play eagerly. [One child represents a breakfast table, another builds a fireplace, a third shows a shepherd followed by his flock, and such activity continues, with each child following his individual interest.] Luncheon follows, after which the children march out of doors singing a marching song. There they dig and weed and plant, water their garden beds, and visit each other . . . an inviting and suitable playground is provided close to the garden. The children rush into the playground, jumping and wrestling, then unite to play games; first a game of bees, which they have just seen hovering over their flowers. Bird games follow, and a flight of pigeons over their heads suggests a pigeon game.[8]

Froebel's reasoning, the basis for the advocacy of such activity by children, is stated in his *The Education of Man:* "A child that plays thoroughly, with self-active determination, perseveringly until physical fatigue forbids, will surely be a thorough determined man, capable of self-sacrifice for the promotion of the welfare of himself and others. Is not the most beautiful expression of child life at this time a playing child?—a child wholly absorbed in his play?—a child that has fallen asleep while so absorbed?"[9] In a letter to a friend, Froebel describes his methods: "The children are treated according to their individuality, and develop freely and naturally in body and mind. The system stimulates their reason and their sense of order and beauty. They enter zealously and heartily into the spirit of the work. Nothing is done for show; everything for the development of the highest in life."[10]

For Froebel nature and education were closely allied. Nature he regarded as a single system, and similarly he maintained that education should deal with all of a child's activities. As noted earlier, Froebel compared a child to a tree which begins as a weak sapling, but, given favorable conditions, will grow into a stalwart giant of the forest.

Before leaving Switzerland, Froebel had begun to invent a series of toys or objects which he called "gifts" and "occupations." The chief aim of the gifts was to guide and motivate children's play and to train them in dexterity of movement and to teach them something about the laws of nature. The gifts consisted of balls, blocks for building, colored tablets for design, colored papers to cut and fold, clay and sand, pencils and paints, arranged in a series. The occupations consisted of paper folding, perforated paper designs for pricking, drawing on squared paper, intertwining, weaving, folding, cutting, peawork, cardboard and clay modeling. These varied devices will be analyzed and described more fully in the following chapter.

A second kindergarten was opened by Froebel in Rudolstadt in 1840, and both Froebel and Middendorff lectured on the scheme in Dresden, Frankfurt, Hamburg, Heidelberg, Darmstadt, Cologne, Stuttgart, Carlsruhe, and elsewhere. Teachers trained at Blankenburg started Froebel schools in Gerau, Hildburghausen, Coburg, and Sondershausen. The system was introduced in an institution for deaf-mutes at Eisenach. Teachers came from various parts of Germany, Hungary, and Belgium to learn Froebel's methods. The training of kindergarten teachers continued at Keilhau, after Blankenburg was closed by lack of funds, and from 1848 to the time of Froebel's death, at Liebenstein in the Thuringian Forest and at Marienthal in the Duchy of Meiningen. The students were mainly young girls, for Froebel had become convinced that young women, because of their strong maternal instincts, when trained for the work made the best teachers of young children.

Concerning ideal qualifications for a kindergarten teacher, Froebel wrote: "Obviously, they must be skilled in those things which are common to both mother and child, since they are to play the part of mediators, so that they can take the place of the mother in caring for and instructing her child; they must therefore be able to lend a hand to the mistress of the house in her housewifely cares, upon emergency, as well as able to relieve her of the burden of watching, attending on, and educating her child. Wherefore such women must be trained in all the work of the house, as well as in the education and care of children."[11]

Froebel agreed with Lessing that "Nature intended woman for her masterpiece." In his later years he devoted his chief attention to women's education. Like Schiller, he felt that the salvation of any country must depend on its women. The principles of evolution in which Froebel believed naturally led him to the woman as the starting point for the child's education. He found sympathy and understanding among women, comparatively little among men. The mother with her infant could best realize his aims and ideals.

Opponents of Froebel's kindergarten theories were numerous in his own time. Some were simply ignorant, others were conservatives who feared any innovation in education. Many were unable to recognize the need for any organized system of education for children under school age. It was also argued that Froebel's emphasis on play would produce loiterers and triflers and unfit the children for the school work to follow. Frank P. Graves, in his *Great Educators of Three Centuries*, replies to such critics: "Froebel's practical work, while at times mechanical, over-schematized, and bolstered by esoteric speculations, is most ingenious, and has enabled society to provide for a neglected and most important stage in education."[12] A key element in Froebel's kindergarten scheme is play. He saw play not merely as recreation, but as the most important phase in the spontaneous development of the child, because it allows him to exercise harmoniously all his physical, emotional, and intellectual qualities.

CHAPTER 6

Gifts and Occupations

THE most striking and original of Froebel's kindergarten methods are associated with what are called "gifts" and "occupations," which the inventor took some fifteen years, 1835 - 50, to conceive, develop, and perfect. The two media are closely connected from the standpoint of use. The "occupations" represent activities while the "gifts" inspire ideas for the activities.

The gifts consist of fundamental forms, comparable to typical formations in nature, designed to show the general qualities of things. Froebel's occupation material includes the following gifts: six soft balls of various colors; sphere, cube, and cylinder made of wood; a large cube, divided into eight small cubes; a large cube, divided into eight oblong blocks; a large cube, consisting of twenty-one whole, six half, and twelve quarter cubes; a large cube, consiting of twenty-one whole, six half, and twelve quarter cubes; a large cube, consisting of eighteen whole oblongs, with three divided lengthwise and six divided breadthwise; quadrangular and various triangular tablets for laying figures; sticks or wands for laying figures; whole and half wire rings for laying figures; material for drawing, perforating, embroidering, paper cutting, weaving or braiding, paper folding, pea work, and modeling, and slats for interlacing.

To assure the constant progress of the child's development, the play-gifts are at first simple and then gradually become more complex, following each other in a natural order of evolution. The knowledge of one is preparation for the next. The first gift of six worsted balls, in six spectrum colors, was intended to become the child's plaything as early as the second month of its existence and from that time on to be used continuously. The ball or sphere, the shape of the world itself, is the simplest of all forms. Besides teaching form, the balls were also intended to teach color, the six

47

balls consisting of three primary and three secondary colors. Froebel and his associates worked out more than one hundred ball games in connection with the first gift. When combined with simple melodies, the balls were the basis for marching, running, jumping, sliding, rolling, twirling, flying, and wandering games. Also a large number of games for the exercise of the limbs and fingers were added, to develop the child's senses and power of attention and independent action. The six woolen balls were to be rolled about in play; and from these actions there would be derived ideas of color, material, form, motion, direction, and muscular control.

The children themselves proved highly inventive in the creation of new games, and Froebel believed that the best kindergarten games came about through following the children's lead. He comments that "the true kindergartners will listen to the suggestions of the children"[1] and will be guided by them. The games should express the child's mind and satisfy his instincts. The kindergarten teacher should beware of doing everything for the child; in fact, by providing suitable objects for play and encouraging suitable action, there may be little need for the teacher to do anything for him.

As the child's powers develop, as he learns to stand, to walk, his games with the ball change; and soon he comes to the stage when a hard noisy ball pleases him more than a soft woolen one. Thus a sphere, cube, and cylinder of hard wood compose the second gift. The stability of the cube is compared with the movability of the sphere, and the two are harmonized in the cylinder, which possesses the powers and characteristics of each. The second gift is the basis of the kindergarten system; all the other gifts are derived from it. The child is expected to use the second gift from the beginning of his second to the conclusion of his third year, while continuing his interest in the first playthings, the colored woolen balls. The sphere, the child discovers, is like the ball in its roundness, but not in its material—wood—nor its hardness.

The third gift was Froebel's response to every child's instinct or desire to pull things to pieces and put them together again. Unlike the preceding three whole bodies, the third, fourth, fifth, and sixth of the play-gifts are building blocks. The third, a large wooden cube divided into eight equal cubes, teaches the relation of the part to the whole and to one another, and makes possible original constructions, such as armchairs, benches, thrones, doorways, monuments, or steps. The three following gifts divide the cube in various ways in order to produce solid bodies of different types and sizes and thus arouse an interest in number, relation, and form, preparing the child's mind for the later study of geometry, algebra, and trigonometry, as well as artistic construction. In the third gift, the cube is divided once in each direction of space, lengthwise, breadthwise, and heightwise, from which what Froebel calls the forms of learning can be derived: the dimensions of length, breadth, and thickness; the meaning of proportions—two halves, four fourths, eight eighths, one whole; the idea of inner and outer; and relationships of size and number. The cube in gift number four is divided into eight oblong blocks; the fifth is one large cube divisible into twenty-one whole, six half, and twelve quarter cubes; the sixth gift consists of eighteen whole oblong blocks, three similar blocks divided lengthwise, and six divided breadthwise, forming altogether one large cube.

As each stage is reached, from the third through the sixth gifts, the variety of forms that can be represented grows greater and in that way gives wider scope to the child's inventive talent. An increase in possible forms and combinations stimulates the child to new efforts toward achieving naturalness and complexity of design in his constructions. Also encouraged in the child are the qualities of order, neatness, economy, and exactness. The social virtues of peacefulness, friendliness, and helpfulness are cultivated; each child uses only his own blocks, taking none from his companions, though an older or more capable child may oversee and assist a younger, less experienced one.

The first series of Froebel's occupation-materials, that is, the first six play-gifts described in the foregoing account, consists of solid bodies. A series following, sometimes referred to as gifts seven to eleven, comprises many plane figures. The building boxes, with their cubular, oblong, and columnar forms, are complemented by plane wooden tablets in the form of squares, and of right, acute, and obtuse-angled triangles in great number. The geometrical forms which the child has already learned from the cubes and oblongs are combined with plane figures to direct the child's attention to surface, bringing out the relation of area to volume. This material offers innumerable opportunities, especially when combined with color, for the invention of symmetrical patterns and artistic design.

Sticks and rings were also used by Froebel. With the sticks, the children could make in outline the shapes to which they had become accustomed to construct from the first gifts and tablets. Here was also the first step toward learning to write; for the sticks, combined with rings or circles, could be laid out to form letters. The process was in harmony with Froebel's belief that the learning process should proceed in logical fashion, each thing learned contributing to the next stage. The occupations of the kindergarten were not expected to advance abruptly, but in accordance with a well-arranged system. The new grows naturally from that which is already known, simply enlarging faculties previously developed.

The occupations, which apply to practice what has been learned through the gifts, comprise a long list of constructions with paper, sand, clay, wood, and other materials. These require greater manual dexterity and include considerable original design. Contrasting with the occupations involving solids in the first six gifts, the more advanced occupations are concerned with clay modeling, cardboard cutting, paper folding, and wood carving, followed by mat and paper weaving, stick shaping, sewing, bead threading, paper pricking, and drawing. In drawing, the child begins with representing the circumference of an actual object. He draws, for example, the outline of a leaf upon a slate, and tries to fill in the veins. Later, he draws a network of lines, forming squares, upon the slate. The lines and angles seen in the cubes, tablets, and sticks also are imitated upon the slate. After drawing squares, right angles, and triangles under the kindergarten teacher's direction, the child is left free to draw according to his own fancy. Self-activity is the first principle of Froebel's method.

In the weaving paper occupation, strips of colored paper are woven into a sheet of differently colored paper with a steel, brass, or wooden needle, according to a systematic plan, to create beautiful small mats. Embroidery, paper folding and cutting, and other occupations are based upon the same principles and skills, further to develop the child's faculties.

It is obvious that Froebel built his entire system of gifts and occupation materials upon mathematical principles. In every case he proceeds from mathematical forms. The child is unaware, of course, of the mathematical significance of his playthings; but his eye unconsciously becomes accustomed to correct mathematical forms. Thus, his senses of form, proportion, and harmony are being developed. Froebel fostered the sense of art in the kindergarten children and also aimed to keep his pupils in perfect harmony with nature through cultivation of their gardens and observation of the nature and habits of small animals.

In the building games and occupations, it was the child's hands that were active. During the years 1840 - 44 Froebel was constantly devising games that would exercise the child's whole body and, at the same time, continue to train his sense of order and observation of nature. For games for both older and younger children, he always began with the ball. The children themselves were quite inventive in imagining new uses of the ball in their games. During the years that he spent at Blankenburg, Froebel was busy creating ball games and other action games, including a variety of games called by the names of natural objects. His series of "movement games" is described in Froebel's *Pedagogics of the Kindergarten,* first published in 1861.

As noted, games were suggested to Froebel by watching the free play of children, originating from childish instincts. The next step was to turn these activities to educational purposes and use them to promote the children's development. Concerning his philosophy of play, Froebel once remarked, "Without rational conscious guidance, childish activity degenerates into aimless play, instead of preparing for those tasks of life to which it is destined to lead."[2] It was not intended, however, that all of a child's play would be under rational direction. Time was allowed in Froebel's kindergarten system for free play, for he clearly understood the value of unrestricted and unregimented play in the child's mental growth.

Another basic aspect of the kindergarten scheme, planned by Froebel and closely related to occupations and games for all children, was music. Long before the Blankenburg establishment, he had begun collecting material for his mother-songs. The songs were tested on Middendorff's children, and they were also circulated to mothers with infants for rigorous preliminary testing. The result was a little collection of nursery songs, issued in 1841. This work developed into the *Mutter- und Kose-lieder* or *Mother's*

Songs, Games and Stories, published in 1843. Froebel himself says of the book: "I have embodied in it the most important ideas of my educational system. It is the starting point for an education according to nature's laws; it shows how all the germs of human endowment have to be nurtured and assisted to produce a full and healthy development."[3]

In the "Family Book," as he called it, Froebel offers mothers a guide for the first stage of the infant's development through physical play exercises. His aim was to persuade mothers that a child's education begins at birth. The songs portray the mother's feeling on the birth of her child, and her hopes and fears as she observes the first movements of its limbs and the evolution of its senses. The *Mother's Songs* are followed by fifty games and songs, each of which has a motto, intended for the mother's guidance, and a verse intended for her to sing to the child. The accompanying music was composed by Froebel's disciple, Robert Kohl. Each game and its song is an exercise for some part of the child's body. In most instances, a picture illustrates the verse. At the end of the book, Froebel supplied commentaries providing additional guidance for mothers using the book.

The rhymes in the *Mother's Songs, Games and Stories* are frequently stiff and stilted and the illustrations of figures and faces somewhat crude, but the book is a tender expression of maternal feeling. It is both a book for mothers and a mother's book, serving as a guide for the mother and harmonizing with her instincts. It shows how the mother, by her love, develops tenderness in the child.

Four groups of games are contained in the *Mother's Songs, Games and Stories*, each representing a stage in the child's development. The first, for the infant in the earliest months of its life, deals with experiences of movement, sense discrimination, imitation, and perception of various objects, especially moving objects. In the second group of games, the child's experience of life is widened; and he learns to classify objects according to their number, form, and size. Here Froebel wanted the mother to train her child's ear in the open air, in the fields and meadows, so that the sounds of nature would become familiar and a source of joy.

A third group of games begins with what are generally known as "light-songs," including "the child and the moon," "the little girl and the stars," "the light bird on the wall," "the window," etc. Froebel suggests that when the child's interest in the moon and stars is first excited, enough should be told him about the heavenly bodies to pave the way for real knowledge later. In the fourth and last stage of the games, Froebel's aim is to make the child realize that he is a member of society and is ready to have his moral sense developed by revealing the distinction between good and bad behavior.

Through all the four series of games, Froebel never neglects his views on the interconnectedness of all things, each stage progressing in logical order from the preceding one. The relationship of the *Mother's Songs, Games and Stories* to the general kindergarten idea is debatable. Some kindergartners assume that it properly belongs to the pre-kindergarten age; others hold that it is practically the core of the kindergarten method. Froebel states that the book is "for the very first training of the child, that is, for mere babyhood; influencing and training the child's body, his limbs and senses, as well as his soul, his mind and his whole inner nature."[4] It is evident, however, that the author expected the work would be handed down as the book of the family and that children of any age would enjoy it as a picture book. A leading educator, William H. Kilpatrick, concludes that "we need not hesitate in supposing that the book is designed to influence children appreciably beyond the kindergarten age."[5]

The strongest feature of Froebel's kindergarten system is his love for and sympathy with childhood. He was almost unique in his time in his respect for the child's individuality. He completely rejected the notion, prevalent in his era, of inherited sin. The child's natural instincts, he held, were proper and worthy of encouragement. The Froebel system was the first to recognize the educative value of play. Building upon this principle, manual and constructive activities were emphasized. Initiative and self-activity were also basic elements of the scheme. Individual expression was emphasized, "For what man tries to represent or to do he begins to understand,"[6] Froebel wrote. Means to this end were provided by building, drawing, modeling, and singing materials.

Another key point in Froebel's teaching is his insistence upon social relationships, beginning with the family as the first social group and continuing through the kindergarten and school. The kindergarten and school, in fact, were simply expected to continue on a broader plane the child's social life already begun in the family—further evidence of Froebel's belief in unity and continuity. Froebel was convinced that the child has a natural inclination toward social intercourse and that social relations are essential to his well-rounded development.

Unique in Froebel's time was his appreciation of the esthetic elements in education. His interest in nature study and school gardens preceded by decades modern practices. His rejection of formal religious instruction was also a radical departure for his era. As Kilpatrick sums up his contributions, "Froebel saw education in far larger terms than the mere memorizing of set intellectual tasks or even the acquiring of the formal school arts. As the embodiment of this vision, the kindergarten will remain a permanent monument to an epochal step in the history of education."[7]

CHAPTER 7

Educational Philosopher

FRIEDRICH Froebel's name is most closely associated with the kindergarten, and it is this institution that has spread his fame. Froebel himself, however, regarded the kindergarten as but one facet of educational reform. His pedagogical system rests upon a philosophical foundation which one must understand in order to appreciate his theories.

Froebel's underlying principles are the outgrowth of the religious influences of his childhood and of his early communion with nature combined with the idealistic philosophy, the Romantic movement, and the scientific spirit of the day. Germany in the early nineteenth century was a nation of poets and thinkers, from whom arose a multitude of conceptions of the place of man in the universe. Froebel was not an adherent of any particular school but was most closely associated with the Romantic movement, personified by Friedrich Schelling, philosopher and university professor. The Romanticism in the literature, art, and religion of the period was mystic in expression and symbolic in thought. For these reasons, Froebel's writings are often vague, emotional, and difficult to comprehend.

Fundamental to Froebel's educational system is his conception of God. For him the goal and the reason for being of education are found in God and the relationship that man and nature bear to the Supreme Being. Some critics have described him as a pantheist, a believer in the doctrine that equates God with the forces and laws of the universe. In the opening paragraph of Froebel's *The Education of Man*, he states his views on the law which governs all life:

In all things there lives and reigns an eternal law. This all controlling law is necessarily based on an all-pervading, energetic, being, self-conscious, and hence eternal, unity. This unity is God. All things have come from the divine Unity, from God, and have their origins in the divine Unity, in God alone. God is the sole source of all things. In all things there lives and reigns a divine Unity, God. All things live and have their being in and through the divine Unity, in and through God. All things are only through the divine effluence that lives in them. The divine effluence that lives in each thing is the essence of each thing.[1]

"It is the special destiny and lifework of man, as an intelligent and rational being," Froebel went on to declare, "to become fully, vividly, and clearly conscious of his essence, of the divine effluence in him, and therefore of God."[2] Thus, as viewed by Froebel, "Education consists in leading man, as a thinking, intelligent being, growing into self-consciousness, to a pure and unsullied, conscious and free representation of the inner law of divine Unity, and in teaching him ways and means thereto." Since "man and nature proceed from God and are conditioned by him," it follows that education should lead "to peace with nature, and to unity with God."[3]

Goodness alone is real, according to Froebel, while evil is a mere distortion of goodness. The educational implication of this belief is that the child is not born evil; on the contrary, any waywardness is usually caused by a lack of vision and the holding of false values. It is the teacher's duty to instruct the child in such a way that the eternal spark of his soul becomes a living reality. Man, nature, and the universe, Froebel maintained, have a fundamental unity; and there was no question in his mind about the moral nature of the universe. To him, the wise man is the good man, for virtue and knowledge are identical. If a child shows any evil traits or serious defects of character and behavior, the only reasonable explanation is that there have been serious mistakes made in his first all-important years.

On this premise, Froebel regarded infancy and the pre-school age as the most significant period for education—exactly the time most neglected in conventional educational practices. Because the child is entirely or mainly under his mother's care during this phase of his life, she is the most important of educators, and needs to be suitably prepared to fulfill her role.

The divine principle in man, assumed by Froebel, is not anything that can be implanted or taught. It is present in every child simply through the origin and nature of man and of the universe and must be left free to develop in unhindered fashion. Any scheme of education that does not base itself on the child's inward growth is fundamentally wrong. An educator who treats the child as "a piece of wax or a lump of clay" to be molded by him is committing a crime against the nature and divinity of the child. The effect of this basic error, Froebel concluded, is disastrous. It cannot change the child's nature, but it can prevent or pervert his true nature from developing. On the reverse, by right understanding, conditions can be provided best to promote the growth of the child's inner nature. Every child must be treated as an individual.

The logical consequence of Froebel's reasoning is that the first condition of all education is full freedom for the child to permit his own living principle of growth to be realized. Only the child who is given the utmost freedom to act, move, and unfold, without constraint or deforming force, can achieve his maximum potential. Play is the fundamental means whereby the child, through his own impulses and inner resources, grows. It is the educator's responsibility to provide the widest opportunity and freedom for such play. The measure of his success will be the child's pleasure and satisfaction in each accomplishment and desire for further achievement. The active child, given free rein, will be continually and eagerly looking and listening, touching, manipulating and exploring, experimenting and discovering. He will engage in every sort of dramatic make-believe and play, by drawing and painting, molding in clay, building with bricks and sand and any other materials at hand, to create things out of his own mind and by his own hands. In such ways, by his own activities, the child forms and educates himself.

Froebel's educational system, in fact, rests broadly on two concepts: the law of self-activity and the law of unity. The underlying principle of all his developing and teaching processes in the kindergarten and in the school was self-activity or spontaneity. Spontaneous self-activity, however, was not intended to mean that the child had to acquire all knowledge by himself without the teacher's aid. Instruction also has a part to play. The creative instinct in the child's mind adapts instruction received in its own way. Thus, as the teacher provides new instruction, the child makes his own use, application, or modification of what he has learned. The child is more interested and more attentive in using than in receiving knowledge. It is more productive for the child to execute his own plan or carry out his own design than to learn passively.

The second fundamental thought in Froebel's scheme was unity: unity in the elements of individual power, physical, intellectual, and spiritual; unity in the exercise of human powers, receptive, reflective, and executive; unity of the race, unity of man with nature, and unity of man with God. The concept of unity led Froebel to insist on complete articulation and the harmonious correlation of studies. In all his educational efforts, he made the idea of unity an essential feature. Every detail of his system of gifts, occupations, games, songs, and stories is marked by this central principle. The unity which characterized the kindergarten as planned by Froebel should, he maintained, be continued in the schools.

In pursuing his favorite theme of organic unity and interconnectedness of all things, Froebel noted that to the superficial observer, nature may appear "as a diversity of many and separate individualities without definite, inner, living connection." But in fact "these externally distinct and separate individualities are organically united members of one great living organism, of one great intrinsically and spiritually coherent whole."[4] Since God is a unity and to Froebel all development is the unfolding of the divine essence, it follows that the whole of the unity works efficiently at every point in the process, as do the component parts: "The essential nature of the whole plant lies in some peculiar manner in each individual part of the plant."[5] "As the germ bears within itself the plant and the whole plant life, does not the child bear also within himself the whole man and the whole life of humanity?"[6] "Does not the whole tree life—indeed the whole vegetable life—work already in each germinating seed of the tree? So, also in each active child, in each activity of the child, works already the totality of the human life—indeed, of the life of humanity?"[7] Froebel's conception of the relation of the individual to society is revealed in the doctrine of the unity and interconnectedness of all things.

As a corollary principle to the idea of interconnectedness, Froebel believed that even in the infant there will be "anticipations" and "premonitions"—that is, a forecast of how the child will develop and what he is destined to become.

Now, having formulated the notion, first, that the universe in general and each entity therein is divine in essence, and second, that this divine essence contains within itself basic or characteristic elements waiting to be unfolded, Froebel goes on to propound his "law of opposities." He insists that "the whole meaning of my educational method rests upon this law alone. The method stands or falls with the recognition or nonrecognition of it. Everything that is left is mere material, the working of which proceeds according to the law, and without that law would not be practicable."[8] Commentators are generally agreed that this is an overstatement, even though the concept has a certain validity. Examples of the application of the law in teaching are demonstrations to the child of the difference between hard and soft, hot and cold, rough and smooth, and, on a more complex level, the sphere and the cube, reading and writing, under and over. When two opposing elements are present, the teacher is to seek a "mediating link" or a "connecting third" to reconcile or harmonize the two; for, according to Froebel, "In nature and in life a third connecting appearance always shows itself between two purely opposite appearances."[9] To illustrate, the cylinder is the link between the sphere and the cube, and speech is the connection between thought and writing. A perceptive critic, William H. Kirkpatrick, concludes, "It appears that Froebel was sadly mistaken in saying that he based his educational practice on the 'law of opposites.' The vital portions of his education are independent of any such mistaken principle."[10]

Another basic Froebel tenet is that education depends on the unity of the family. A home united by love is the best institution for human progress. Association with family and friends is an important factor in moral education. Therefore, children should be reared in a wholesome environment and learn ideals of cooperation at an early stage. The primary significance of play activities to Froebel was that the child in playing reveals his inner nature and simultaneously develops into a social being. The child's growth as seen by Froebel is a continuous and cumulative affair from the beginning, and it is vital to shield the growing child from everything likely to impede or distort his wholesome development. The essential human elements, each of whom should play a part, are educators who can see the whole man at every stage from infancy onward, properly trained helpers who will dedicate themselves to the task, and mothers who understand the power and the privilege that are theirs and will act accordingly.

The child from its birth onward, according to Froebel's conclusion, needs a sense of companionship and close communion with those around him. As a member of a family, he desires the feeling of family unity—with his mother, father, brothers, and sisters. He is also brought into relationship with other children and soon wants to engage in play activities with them. Gradually, such connections extend to other adults and to larger groups of the school and the community. The child's horizon is thus broadened from the family to the community and finally to the society of mankind. The educator bears the responsibility of arranging for his pupils to join congenial playmates and eventually to enter larger communities of fellow learners, fellow players, and fellow workers.

Froebel placed great emphasis on his theory of development. As he saw it, the early period in a child's life is absolutely vital to the full realization of his potentialities. In his study of science, Froebel was impressed by the fact that in every part of organic nature, life and growth appeared to be a progressive development from lower to higher grades of being. The exercise of function was observed to produce development, while failure to exercise checked or destroyed it. In dealing with young human beings, Froebel concluded, the wisest course to follow, especially in the earliest years, is to try to develop human nature's inborn original capacities and abilities by a carefully planned, graduated, and connected program in every direction in which progress is desired. This means helping the child's normal growth, providing a proper environment, and supplying the best means for the activities which the child's nature requires for development. All aspects of education interfering with natural evolution are to be proscribed. "God does not cram in or ingraft," Froebel maintains, in the concluding section of *The Education of Man;* "he develops the smallest and most imperfect thing in continuously ascending stages and in accordance with eternal laws grounded in and developing from the thing's own self."[11]

The purpose of the curriculum, Froebel held, is to develop perception. Facts are incidental and memorization is to be avoided. Only direct experience with life and the world at large makes a definite impact on an individual. Of special concern to Froebel is the matter of creativity. Does one become creative because of inner or outer forces? Does creativity come spontaneously or in response to discipline? It is natural for everyone to aim at self-expression and self-realization—a characteristic of all ages. At the most elementary level, a child builds a sand castle, while the adult scientist or engineer may be testing a revolutionary new theory or erecting a skyscraper. If the creative impulse is encouraged and fostered in the child, Froebel believed, his mature years are likely to be marked by above ordinary creativity and inventiveness.

Froebel defines the primary goal of education in idealistic, mystically romantic terms:

The debasing illusion that man works, produces, creates only in order to preserve his body, in order to secure food, clothing, and shelter, may have to be endured, but should not be diffused and propagated. Primarily and in truth man works only that his spiritual, divine essence may assume outward form, and that thus he may be enabled to recognize his own spiritual, divine nature and the innermost being of God. Whatever food, clothing and shelter he obtains thereby comes to him as an insignificant sur-plus. . . . Yet human power should be developed, cultivated, and manifested not only in inner repose, as religion and religious spirit; not only in outward efficiency, as work and industry; but also—withdrawing upon itself and its own resources—in abstinence, temperance, and frugality.[12]

By way of summary, the fundamental principles which underlie Froebel's educational doctrines are as follows: the conception of God as the source and essence of the world as a whole and of every organic thing in it; development as a universal law to be achieved through children's self-activity, in the guidance of which continuity and connectedness must be maintained; recognition of the impor-tance of the pre-school age in determining a child's character; and the need for guidance to insure that the child will form proper habits of thinking, acting, and feeling.

Pervading all of Froebel's teachings and writings are a love for and sympathy with childhood. He respected the individuality of the child and totally rejected the prevalent religious doctrine of total depravity. For him, the child's interests are proper and worthy of encouragement. Froebel was the first important educator to see the educational advantages of play. Initiative on the part of the child also received special attention. A major feature of Froebel's system, too, is insistence upon social relationships. The child's natural in-clination toward social intercourse, beginning in the family, should be continued, Froebel believed, in the kindergarten and school. Here again, the principles of unity and continuity are to rule.

CHAPTER 8

Froebel As Writer

FRIEDRICH Froebel was a prolific writer, though the majority of his contributions on education are brief. Not more than two or three of his works can be rated as major: *The Education of Man; Mother's Songs, Games and Stories;* and perhaps *Pedagogics of the Kindergarten.* The first collected edition of Froebel's writings ran to three volumes: *Gesammelte Paedagogische Schriften,* edited by Wichard Lange (Berlin, 1862).

Froebel's first published essay, "On the Universal German Educational Institute of Rudolstadt," appeared in 1822 while the author was principal of the Keilhau school. Another pamphlet, "On German Education, Especially as Regards the Universal German Education Institute at Keilhau," came out the same year. The following year, Froebel printed "Christmas at Keilhau, a Christmas Gift to the Parents of the Pupils at Keilhau, to the Friends and Members of the Institute."

An editor of a selection of Froebel's writings, Irene M. Lilley, points out, quite perceptively, that Froebel "seldom wrote in order to explain ideas in general terms. The outpouring of voluminous letters was a continuous monologue in which he developed and elaborated his beliefs. Almost all the works which he published were occasional pieces—pamphlets or letters which made specific appeals for support of his schemes, or articles which described particular aspects and details of his methods. Compilers and translators later on gave to his miscellaneous writings an ordered form which they did not in origin possess."[1]

I   The Education of Man

Froebel's first full-scale written exposition of his educational principles and theories was published in 1826: *The Education of Man,* subtitled *The Art of Education, Instruction and Training Aimed at the Educational Institute at Keilhau*—generally acknowledged to be his most important work.

The difficulties of Froebel's style in this, the most famous of his writings and the only general educational treatise he ever attempted, are evident throughout. It is characteristic of the author that he left the book unfinished, in part because of the vastness of the subject and partly because he was unable or unwilling to devote the concentrated attention to it which the task would have required. In common with Froebel's other writings, *The Education of Man* was privately printed, a fact which severely limited its circulation; but it is doubtful that any commercial publisher would have risked issuing it without a subsidy. The work was never popular; and it is unlikely that many persons have read it from cover to cover, even though it is widely quoted. As Lilley noted, in all Froebel's writings "there are formidable difficulties of presentation and meaning. His style is verbose, repetitive, convoluted. There are long rhetorical passages, peculiar word-plays and eccentric emphases. He would never listen to criticism, or use the accepted philosophical terms."[2]

Nevertheless, *The Education of Man* contains the main clues to Froebel's educational thought. Herein are found the views which he formed at the beginning of his educational career and also the seminal ideas later developed for the education of young children. Actually, the assumptions stated by Froebel in *The Education of Man* and other early writings remained basically unchanged for the remainder of his life. That fact is in accord with his philosophical belief in the continuity of an individual's growth. Introspection was a marked characteristic of Froebel's mind. In his *Autobiography* he concedes that "The fundamental characteristics of my life from the very first have been unceasing self-contemplation, self-analysis and self-education, and they have remained so to this day."[3]

The Education of Man is essentially a statement of what Froebel thought that education should mean. He begins by presenting his general conception of the universe and of the meaning of man's life therein. Next, he proceeds to explain, illustrate, and apply several of his leading principles, in some instances attempting to establish their psychological basis, following the human being, more or less systematically, through childhood, boyhood, and youth. Finally,

Froebel deals with the chief subjects of school instruction and how they should be taught, though at this stage his views in that area were still in a somewhat embryonic state. The major portion of *The Education of Man* is devoted to an analysis of the pupil's development in the first years of school age and an examination of the school in terms of the needs of the child's nature and of the broad fields of knowledge which must be opened to him.

As a pantheistic Christian, Froebel insisted upon the constant presence and operation of God in the universe. Since he believed that all things live and have their being in and through God, everything in Froebel's mind becomes a symbol. For example, in section 69 of *The Education of Man*, the sphere becomes the symbol of diversity in unity and unity in diversity, and other abstract ideas. In Froebel's words, "the spherical or, in general, the round form is most commonly the first and the last form of things in nature: e.g., the great heavenly bodies, such as the suns, planets, and moons, water and all liquids, the air and all gases, and even the dust."[4] In the following sections, 70 - 72, Froebel finds strange sermons in the faces and edges of crystals, and in section 73 many mystic meanings are associated with plants and flowers. Such farfetched symbolism bears little relation to the fundamental educational principles presented in *The Education of Man* and tends to confuse rather than enlighten.

Great stress is placed by Froebel on his theory of development or evolution at every stage of life. Froebel was the first fully to apply the theory to education and to translate it into action. Development is seen as the growth from germ to complete organism. Furthermore, development occurs through exercise of function, that is, by use of one's functions. As seen by Froebel, neglect or disease of any part of an organism leads to its dwindling or gradual weakening, and perhaps even the disappearance of that part. Heredity is viewed as an important factor in development, due to what Froebel describes as the connectedness of humanity. Through successive generations, a given faculty or organ may shrink away or be brought to greater perfection, depending upon exercise. Humanity past, present, and future is one continuous whole, according to Froebel. If development of the hand, the body, or the mind is desired, the answer is suitable exercise. Similarly, if the whole human being is to be developed, the entire human being must be exercised, principally by way of self-activity in harmony with the nature of the individual.

Based on this premise, Froebel sees education as a continuous whole, each part related to every other part, with each element aiding and advancing every other element. Isolated, unrelated facts do not become knowledge until they are compared, classified, organized, and connected. The concept of creativeness combined with the principle of self-activity and the doctrines of continuity and connectedness form the heart of Froebel's system, as presented in *The Education of Man*. The constant theme of the work is the application of the law of evolution to education and how the development of the whole human being is to be achieved. Froebel addresses the book to both teachers and parents.

The second part of *The Education of Man* discusses "The chief groups of subjects of instruction," beginning with religion and religious instruction. Froebel emphasizes the need for the early cultivation of religion in the child, but work and religion must be combined; for, he states, "Religion without industry, without work, is liable to be lost in empty dreams, worthless visions, idle fancies."[5] Proceeding from his profound faith, Froebel insists that "the school should first of all teach the religion of Christ; it should first of all, and above all, give instruction in the Christian religion."[6]

Second in importance in Froebel's scheme of education is nature study. Nature and religion in his mind are inseparable. "For nature, as well as all existing things, is a manifestation, a revelation, of God,"[7] he declares. Only a truly religious person, Froebel believed, "can possibly attain a true understanding and a living knowledge of nature; only such a one can be a genuine naturalist."[8] No study, he thought, aroused such a close feeling of sympathy between pupils and teachers as the thoughtful study of nature and the objects of nature. The guidance of mature minds, however, is an essential condition; for without the guidance designed to show the students "the integrity of nature as a continuously self-developing whole," a child's interest in animals and insects may degenerate into cruelty. Froebel advocated further that nature be viewed whole rather than from any piecemeal or fragmentary approach.

In connection with nature study, Froebel treats of mathematics. He regarded number, form, and magnitude as inseparably connected. Mathematics, he maintains, "mediates, unites, generates knowledge . . . it is a living whole. . . . Mathematics is neither foreign to actual life nor something deduced from life; it is an expression of life as such; therefore its nature may be studied in life, and life may be studied with its help."[9] Froebel concludes with the assertion that "Education without mathematics (at least a thorough knowledge of number, supplemented by occasional instruction in form and magnitude) is, therefore, weak, imperfect patchwork; it interposes insuperable limits to the normal culture and development of man . . . the mind and mathematics are as inseparable as the soul and religion."[10]

Instruction in languages, Froebel held, must be closely connected with the teaching of religion and with nature study. Religion, natural science, and language, in his view, form an integral unity. None of these branches of instruction is independent of the others: "A complete knowledge and firm confidence in the one necessarily implies complete knowledge and firm confidence in the other; a true study of the one necessarily implies also the true study of the other."[11] Here again Froebel applies his principles of continuity and connectedness or correlation of studies. Like Comenius and Pestalozzi before him, he thinks that in teaching languages, care should be taken to connect words with real ideas of the things and objects named. Language is thus brought to life, and its study promotes the conception of concrete ideas. Though Froebel advocated the memorizing of religious sayings and of poems about nature, these were regarded simply as giving expression to feelings already present in the child's mind.

In his discussion of writing, Froebel takes a retrospective look at the early history of the race, noting that the desire for pictorial and symbolic expression led to pictorial hieroglyphics and eventually to alphabetic letters. Froebel has been criticized for postponing too long the teaching of writing and reading. His answer is:

Writing and reading, which necessarily imply a living knowledge of language to a certain extent, lift man beyond every other known creature and bring him nearer the realization of his destiny. Through the practice of these arts he attains personality. The endeavor to learn these arts makes the scholar and the school. . . . Since reading and writing are of such great importance to man, the boy (when he begins to practice them) should possess a sufficient amount of strength and insight. He must be ready for selfconsciousness and must have already experienced the need and desire to know them before he begins to learn these arts.[12]

Finally, in his scheme of pedagogy, Froebel turns to a consideration of the educational value of art—singing, drawing, painting, and modeling. His aim is not to train artists, but to awaken the ideal side of human nature as a means to full, all-round development and to produce in the young a feeling and perception of beauty in order that they may appreciate the masterpieces of the human spirit.

In the last portion of *The Education of Man*, a total of about 2 hundred pages, Froebel considers the "Connection between the School and the Family and the Subjects of Instruction It Implies." Here he develops in some depth his theories of continuity, connectedness, and creativeness; the uses of games and stories; and the place of formal studies, such as arithmetic, geometry, grammatical exercises, writing, and reading. The central objective always is well-rounded development, to be achieved through the pupil's self-activity, guided by the principles of continuity and connectedness.

The Education of Man is concerned mainly with Froebel's ideas on the education of children beyond the kindergarten age, from seven to fourteen. At the time of the book's publication, 1826, no distinct vision of the kindergarten had yet entered Froebel's mind. *The Education of Man* is by no means a final statement of the author's educational views. As one of Froebel's biographers, H. C. Bowen, points out, "he went on modifying and improving to the very last month of his life. His educational system was not looked on by him as a stationary, completed thing, a stereotyped plan to be handed from one to another, and to be reproduced with mechanical, unchanging imitation; nor as a light and airy fancy which any gentle heart can build on a summer's afternoon,—the sole prerequisites for which are liveliness and a love of children."[13]

II   Mother's Songs, Games and Stories

Froebel's second major work, *Mutter-und Kose-lieder*, translated as *Mother's Songs, Games and Stories*, was first published in 1843, several years after the opening of the first kindergarten and some seventeen years after *The Education of Man*. The contents and nature of this work have been previously reviewed. The book contains songs and finger plays for the occupation of mother and child, accompanied by pages of complex, rather crude illustrations; prefatory remarks in rhyme; and long prose explanations of the purpose and symbolic meaning of the activities. Each game and song, picture and commentary, is designed to form a complete unit.

The *Mother's Songs* was one of the results of three years' experience in the kindergartens of Blankenburg, Rudolstadt, and Gera, as well as of the experience and thinking of preceding years. A leading commentator, William H. Kilpatrick, notes that "No other of Froebel's books has occasioned so much dispute."[14] It is described by Froebel himself as a book for mothers and families "for the very first training of the child, that is, for mere babyhood."[15] Some kindergartners, while faithful to Froebel's system, have made small use of the *Mother's Songs*, in the belief that it properly belongs to the pre-kindergarten age. Others insist that it is practically the heart of the kindergarten method. In any case, the book represents the acme of Froebel's concern for the very young child.

In Kilpatrick's opinion, "If we confine our attention to the general statement of Froebel's thought and idea, the pedagogical purpose of the Mother Play book is sound. It is essentially an effort to note the child's instinctive reactions and to utilize these to the realization of the social ideal. Play, the natural play of childish nature and endeavor, is to serve as a medium both for discovering to the observer the natural interests and for leading these to their proper social goal."[16] A close examination of the book must convince one that the *Mother's Songs* is meant for mothers rather than for kindergartners, despite the fact that Froebel stated the book should form "the basis of kindergarten teaching"; he evidently hoped that it would be "handed down from mother to children's children as the book of the family,"[17] a picture book for the child of any age. As in other Froebel works, critics object to excessive use of symbolism and metaphor, which leads Kilpatrick to conclude that "the Mother Play book as a whole is not a safe book to put in the hands of mothers or of kindergarten novitiates," who "would surely be misled if they followed its teachings."[18] Though Kilpatrick concedes that the intelligent kindergartner may find useful suggestions in the work, he concludes that "it seems reasonably clear that the rank and file of practical kindergartners had better spend their time exclusively on more valuable books."[19]

A new version of the *Mother's Songs,* entitled *The Mottoes and Commentaries of Friedrich Froebel's Mother Play,* assembled and translated by Susan E. Blow, was published in 1895. The aim was to clarify Froebel's thought and "to avoid so far as possible the tautologies, involutions, and circumlocutions of his obscure and labored style."[20] Both prose and poetic versions of the mottoes are presented.

III   Pedagogics of the Kindergarten

The third and last of Froebel's principal writings, *Pedagogics of the Kindergarten, or His Ideas Concerning the Play and Playthings of the Child* was published posthumously in Berlin in 1861. The work consists of fiteen Froebel essays, collected and edited by Wichard Lange. It bears a close relationship to the *Mother's Songs,* but is less lively and readable than the latter, tending to be expository and dry and going into wearisome detail. The *Pedagogics of the Kindergarten* devotes most of its three hundred-plus pages to Froebel's "gifts and occupations" previously described. Separate chapters deal with each of the gifts or playthings, beginning with the ball, the sphere, and the cube, and how they should be utilized in the child's education. A series of plates illustrates graphically the manipulation of the various objects. In addition to the educational playthings, Froebel selected other means of occupying children such as drawings, paper plaiting, paper folding, paper cutting, and paper pricking, and modeling in sand and clay; these, too, are suitably illustrated. The gifts formed an elaborate sequence, but Froebel justified them with the contention that they were learned and adopted from watching the children's own behavior. He found an educational value in every phase of the children's play.

The final essay contained in the *Pedagogics,* "How Lina Learned to Read and Write," indicates what Froebel expected of a child whose self-activity had been properly developed in a good kindergarten. The lesson of self-help, he concludes, is the most important one to be learned by the pupils in a school.

IV *Autobiography*

In the belief that self-examination and self-consciousness are essential to the complete development of every human being, Froebel wrote at length of his own career and the influences which had been instrumental in its shaping. He claimed that self-contemplation, self-analysis, and self-education had been a lifelong trait in his character.

Froebel left at least three autobiographical accounts. In the *Letter to the Duke of Meiningen,* written in 1827, he justifies himself as an educator by reflecting on the meaning of his own experiences as a child and youth and the nature of his preparation for the teaching profession. Froebel had intended to present this statement to the Duke of Meiningen during the negotiations concerning the proposed National Educational Institution at Helba, for which the Duke's financial support was sought. As noted earlier, the plea failed because of jealousy of Froebel among the Duke's advisers. The *Letter* survives only in rought draft; apparently it was never finished, properly corrected, or polished into permanent form; and it was probably never delivered to the person to whom it was addressed.

A year after the communication intended for the Duke, Froebel wrote a second autobiographical narrative, addressed to the philosopher Karl Krause, with whom he was engaged in friendly controversy. Again he analyzed the main factors in his intellectual growth and the route by which he arrived at his view of life. Three years later, in 1831, Froebel drafted a third, perhaps the most revealing, of his personal revelations, the *Letter to the Women in Keilhau.* At the time, he was involved in a deep emotional crisis because of the seeming failure of the Keilhau experiment and the complex problems of his relationships with the staff there. Thus the *Letter to the Women of Keilhau* is an agonizing appraisal of Froebel's personal struggle.

Throughout these several autobiographical statements, Froebel reflected on his own childhood and adolescent years, trying to identify the elements in his surroundings which hindered or encouraged personal development. Clearly there was much in the early years to impede his growth: the harsh indifference of a stepmother, neglect by a busy, stern father, and a rigid religious atmosphere. At the same time, the mystical and symbolic language of the hymns and sermons which he constantly heard made a permanent impress on Froebel's thought and later writing and teaching.

The unhappy, repressive first decade of Froebel's life was followed by five peaceful years spent in his uncle's quiet clerical home at Stadt Ilm, where he came under the guidance of sympathetic adults and associated with schoolboys of his own age. His subsequent apprenticeship to a forester also played a significant part in shaping Froebel's mind, bringing him into what he called "religious communion with nature." The next seventeen years were spent by Froebel in a restless search for a congenial career, a period which covered his stays at the universities of Jena, Göttingen, and Berlin, and military service during Germany's war of liberation. All of his basic ideas, later applied to the field of education, were acquired by Froebel during this formative period.

The autobiographies briefly described above end more than twenty years prior to Froebel's death and therefore omit the Swiss sojourn, 1831 - 1835, and more importantly, the development of the kindergarten. For those events, we must rely upon such documents, written by Froebel, as *Plans for an Institution for the Education of the Poor in the Canton of Berne* (1833), articles in the *Sunday Journal* on play material (1838 - 40), and *Outline of a Plan for Founding and Developing a Kindergarten* (1840) together with contemporary biographies, such as the Baroness Berthe Maria von Marenholtz-Bülow's *Reminiscences of Friedrich Froebel* and Johannes Barop's *Critical Moments in the Froebel Community*. During the past century a vast body of Froebellian literature has grown up in book and periodical form, as changing interpretations of Froebel's significance in the world of education have proliferated.

CHAPTER 9

Associates and Disciples

THE propagation of Froebel's theories and teachings on the early education of children was vastly aided by a corps of devoted associates and disciples, among whom Wilhelm Middendorff, Heinrich Langethal, Baroness Berthe von Marenholtz-Bülow, Johannes Barop, Wichard Lange, and Froebel's second wife, Luise Levin Froebel, stand out.

As noted earlier, Froebel's acquaintance and friendship with Middendorff and Langethal began in 1813 during his brief military career in the Prussian army. The relationship of Middendorff to Froebel has been compared to that of Aaron to Moses in the Exodus story. Like the Biblical Moses, Froebel was "slow of speech and of a slow tongue," and like Aaron, Middendorff was "his spokesman unto the people." It was Middendorff's clearness and eloquence of speech which won adherents for Froebel among people who neither knew him nor could understand him. From the beginning, Middendorff was irresistibly attracted by Froebel's character and ideas and remained intensely loyal to him throughout his life.

The careers of Froebel and Middendorff are so interwoven that separation is difficult. Middendorff was the first of Froebel's friends to join him in an educational enterprise—the Universal German Educational Institute at Griesheim, later transferred to Keilhau, 1816 - 17. Middendorff, the son of a prosperous farmer in Westphalia, was a student in theology, who had expected to enter the ministry in his home parish. But inspired by Froebel with a new ideal of education, Middendorff abandoned the clergyman's calling to be a teacher. In her *Reminiscences of Friedrich Froebel*, Baroness Berthe von Marenholtz-Bülow eulogies Middendorff's character in the highest terms. His nature, she writes, was "to conquer all opposition with love, to harmonize discords, to veil faults

72

when they could not be cured, to see the better side in dark days, to trust the all-powerful Providence with pious devotion."[1]

Middendorff shared Froebel's deep interest in natural history and love of the outdoors. One of his favorite occupations was rambling through the Keilhau valley with boys in the school, leading them through pine forests from which they emerged to view spectacular mountains and valleys below. Middendorff interested the children in the neighborhood by relating to them stories and legends associated with the area and the origins of place names. In the course of their hikes, the boys discovered various delicious wild berries growing on the hills; collected, pressed, and named all the flowers of the neighborhood; and studied the animals and insects of the field.

Middendorff was not a writer and apparently disliked to write. His forte was the spoken word, a born orator. His great service to Froebel was his unselfish dedication to the practical realization of Froebel's ideas and the magnetic influence of his oral expositions, on numerous occasions, of the Froebel principles. His few published works included *Thoughts on the Kindergarten,* addressed in 1848 to the German Parliament. Therein he replies to several questions about the place of the kindergarten in the educational scheme. To the inquiry, "Why must the kindergarten be?" Middendorff responds that parents have neither the knowledge nor the leisure to look after the early development of the child's mental and physical faculties. Thus the trained kindergartner is needed to compensate for indifference, ignorance, or perversity on the part of parents or nurses at a critical period in the child's life. To the next query, "How is a kindergarten carried on?" Middendorff describes briefly the whole process of child culture from the baby play and song to the later occupations. For skeptics who questioned the effect of the kindergarten on the child, Middendorff invited parents to visit a kindergarten in operation to see for themselves the development of the child's whole being.

Middendorff's rapport with his pupils was perfect. He was as much a companion and friend of the boys as a teacher. He entered into animated conversation with the children about anything that interested them and, as noted, shared their rambles. Middendorff took pleasure in stimulating the children's imagination, while Froebel aimed rather to develop their reason and intelligence.

Froebel's educational ventures in Switzerland owed much of their success to Middendorff. The latter went with Froebel to Wartensee in 1831 to start a school in the Canton of Lucerne. After the transfer to Willisau, Middendorff served as director of the school for several years without once taking leave to visit his family back in Keilhau. "I did not dare to stir at this time," he commented later. "I was guarding, as it were, an outpost of our stronghold. As long as the Catholic clergy persisted in their hostilities, it was impossible to leave even for the sake of my dear ones. And yet, I can hardly understand now how I did it."[2] Here was another striking instance of Middendorff's devotion and loyalty to Froebel.

When Froebel died in June 1852, his monument, in the form of a column with cube, cylinder, and ball, and inscribed with Goethe's words, "Come let us live for our children," was designed by Middendorff. For the remainder of his life (he survived Froebel by only eighteen months), Middendorff's efforts were directed toward establishing Froebel's work on a solid basis. His first object was to complete the training course for kindergarten teachers at Marienthal, which Froebel had left unfinished. The Keilhau community was keenly aware of the need for sending out as many well-trained and competent kindergarten teachers as possible. Effective presentation of the kindergarten idea was also made by Middendorff at education conferences, shortly before his death in November, 1853.

The second of Froebel's co-workers, in chronological order, was Heinrich Langethal, who had been a student of theology at Berlin before he and Froebel met in the 1812 - 13 war against Napoleon. Langethal was barely twenty-one years of age at the time. After the war, Langethal completed his studies at the University of Berlin and then came to Keilhau to visit his old comrades-in-arms. So impressed was Langethal with the Keilhau institution that he decided to remain as a teacher, adding much strength to the small faculty. In the summer of 1826 both Middendorff and Langethal were married, the former to the oldest daughter of Christian Froebel, and Langethal to the adopted daughter of Friedrich Froebel's wife.

Langethal apparently possessed qualities that were lacking in Froebel and Middendorff. He had an excellent background of classical knowledge, combined with great teaching ability. He was also a gifted musician. His reputation as a scientist and his Berlin connection brought several pupils to the school. Langethal's first efforts were to cure the boys of their ugly Thuringian accent and to teach them correct German. He was also their leader in various strenuous games and in mountain climbing. In language studies, Langethal began with Greek, followed by Latin, accepting Herbart's order of teaching the classical languages.

After Froebel's return to Germany, Langethal went to Switzerland to replace him as director of the Burgdorf school. Afterward, Langethal resigned to take charge of a girls' school at Berne.

A later Froebel associate was Johannes Arnold Barop, a nephew of Middendorff and a divinity student at Halle, who came to visit the Keilhau school in 1823 (at age twenty-one) and decided to remain as a teacher, much to his family's displeasure. Eventually Barop became the mainstay of the whole enterprise, as has been previously described.

During Froebel's Swiss sojourn, when he was struggling to establish a school, first at Wartensee and then at Willisau, Barop came on from Keilhau to join him and remained in Switzerland for more than a year. Barop was a courageous individual and responded vigorously to the Catholic clergy's attacks on Froebel and his school. Barop was especially the object of suspicion, his black coat giving him the appearance of one of the Protestant heretic clergy. Typical of a number of incidents was an occurrence in an inn as Barop was on his way to Lucerne. A priest seeing him, violently denounced the "God-forgotten heretic." At last Barop rose slowly, according to the account, walked steadily toward his angry critic, and asked, "Do you know, sir, who Jesus Christ was, and have you any respect for Him?" Confused by the quiet firmness of his manner, the priest answered, "Yes, certainly; he is God's Son, and we must believe in him and honor Him, unless we wish to be damned eternally." Barop continued, "Perhaps you can tell me whether Christ was a Catholic or a Protestant?" The priest remained silent. The question won over the audience, who applauded Barop, and the priest fled.[3]

At the conclusion of his Swiss mission, in 1832, Barop returned to Keilhau as director of the school. By his skill, energy, and good management, he was able in a few years to bring back prosperity to the parent establishment, to pay off its debts, and to give assistance to other branches of the community. Barop lived on for many years after Froebel, Middendorff, and other early associates; he came into a rich inheritance and enjoyed many honors. The University of Jena conferred a doctor's degree on him at its jubilee, and the Prince of Rudolstadt appointed him minister of education.

An effective publicist for Froebel's work was Wichard Lange, who came to know Froebel when the latter visited Hamburg in the winter of 1849 - 50. Lange served as editor of Froebel's *Weekly Journal*. About ten years after Froebel's death, Lange collected and edited an edition of Froebel's writings. Further, Lange was a frequent contributor to the *Educational Journal (Die Rheinischen Blatter)*, founded by Diesterweg. In the large boys' school which he long conducted at Hamburg, Lange introduced Froebellian principles. His connection with the Froebel community was strengthened also by his marriage to Middendorff's daughter.

Froebel's second marriage, in July 1851, to Luise Levin occurred only a year before his death. She joined Middendorff in teaching the training class at Marienthal, instructing the students in "occupations," while Middendorff was teaching the kindergarten theory. Of her, the Baroness Berthe von Marenholtz-Bülow writes: "Although deeply afflicted by the sad, irreparable loss of her husband after only one year's married life, she fulfilled the task, now become so much more difficult, with the greatest conscientiousness, firmly resolved to devote her whole strength to it in order to preserve and promote the work already begun. At the same time she remained an affectionate, motherly friend and guardian of the pupils."[4]

In 1854 Frau Froebel was asked by the principal of a kindergarten in Hamburg to supply a teacher. She responded by taking one of her students there to start her in the work. At Hamburg, Frau Froebel found such fertile ground for her educational efforts that she remained to start a kindergarten and training school of her own, along with transition and preparatory classes. She also organized the first kindergarten in Berlin under the management of two of Froebel's best students and with Adolph Diesterweg founded a Kindergarten Union, of which she became the president. She was still actively employed at Hamburg in the kindergarten cause as late as 1886, thirty-three years after Froebel's death.

The most able and influential exponent of Froebel's work, before and after his decease, was the Baroness Berthe von Marenholtz-Bülow, who had been married while still in her teens to Baron von Marenholtz, a member of the privy council and later court marshal of Hanover. The Baroness devoted herself to the education of her one son and her husband's children by a former marriage. She was a woman of influence, fluent in several languages, and gifted with a pleasing personality. Always a student of the best methods of education and well educated herself, the Baroness was immediately receptive to the kindergarten idea. Her first meeting with Froebel occurred in 1849 while visiting the Baths at Liebenstein, where Froebel was training a class of young women to become kindergarteners.

At the time, Froebel had gained some notoriety for the lack of self-consciousness with which he played games with the children of the neighborhood. In her *Reminiscences of Friedrich Froebel*, the Baroness has an amusing and touching account of their first meeting:

My landlady told me that a few weeks before, a man had settled down on a small farm near the springs, who danced and played with the village children, and therefore went by the name of "the old fool." Some days after I met on my walk this so-called "old fool." A tall, spare man, with long gray hair, was leading a troop of village children between the ages of three and eight, most of them barefooted and but scantily clothed, who marched two and two up a hill, where, having marshalled them for a play, he practiced with them a song belonging to it. The loving patience and *abandon* with which he did this, the whole bearing of the man while the children played various games under his direction, were so moving, that tears came into my companion's eyes as well as into my own, and I said to her, "This man is called an 'old fool' by these people; perhaps he is one of those men who are ridiculed or stoned by contemporaries, and to whom future generations build monuments."[5]

Thenceforth the Baroness devoted herself for the remainder of a long lifetime to the propagation and spread of the kindergarten movement through her writing and lecturing. In 1854, six months were spent in England; while there she published a pamphlet in English on *Infant Gardens*. The Baroness is reported to have horrified her family by carrying on propaganda abroad in a period when women of the upper classes were not accustomed to travel alone or to stay in hotels and when it was rare for a woman to speak in public. Accompanied, however, by a friend and later by a niece, she carried out a series of lecture tours.

Following the journey to England, the Baroness crossed to Paris and remained in France for three years. There were already some French crèches in existence; and at one of these the patroness, the Empress Eugénie, allowed a trial to be made of Froebel's methods. After three months, an investigating committee submitted a favorable report. Accordingly, during the second year of the Baroness' stay the "Comité du Patronage des Jardins d'Enfants" was founded.

In 1857 - 58 the Baroness transferred her missionary work to Belgium, where a flourishing kindergarten was in operation under the direction of Madame Guillaume, a kindergarten teacher from Hamburg who had married in Brussels. The Belgian authorities were persuaded by the Baroness to let her introduce Froebel's occupations in the primary schools. A year later she was in Holland "enlisting new disciples and encouraging those who had already embraced the new ideas." She pronounced the Dutch kindergartens the best that she had seen. Switzerland was the next stop; there the Baroness lectured at Geneva, Neufchatel, and Lausanne. On an earlier occasion she had visited Zurich. Froebel's previous efforts had apparently left no permanent impress on the Swiss, but in the late eighteen-fifties the system was being reintroduced.

Several years later the Baroness visited Italy. Italians had met her earlier in Paris and Switzerland, articles about her had been read in Swiss papers, and the "gifts" and "occupations" had been introduced in North and South Italy, though in some cases the material had been adopted with limited understanding of the guiding principles. Kindergartens had been established in Rome, Naples, Palermo, Milan, and Venice, and in Chambéry and Nice in the former Duchy of Savoy. The Italian journey was the last long lecture tour undertaken by the Baroness. Increasing age made it necessary for her to spend most of her time in Germany, principally at the training institute which she had established at Dresden. Both European and American educators interested in kindergarten work visited her there.

The Baroness died in 1893. Her niece, who wrote her biography, noted that she looked back "from the height of her completed career on the established position and prospects of the New Education, to which she had devoted her life. Wherever she looked in Europe the words 'Froebel's kindergarten' were not an empty sound, but had long ago become a fact—a recognized fact. Then she looked across the ocean to America and the kindergarten triumphed there."[6]

Despite her work in foreign lands, the Baroness' principal contributions to the kindergarten cause were made in Germany. She was instrumental in starting a journal called *The Education of the Future;* she wrote the authoritative biography *Reminiscences of Friedrich Froebel;* she took the lead in removing the restrictions on kindergartens in Prussia; founded an Association for Home Education in Berlin, the purposes of which are explained in her book *Work and the New Education According to Froebel;* and she inspired the establishment of a number of kindergartens in Berlin, Dresden, and elsewhere. The Baroness was also a prolific writer on kindergarten subjects—Henry Barnard's *Papers on Froebel's Kindergarten* lists fourteen substantial works from her pen from 1849 to 1877.[7]

An examination of the history of the kindergarten movement reveals clearly the indispensable role played by Froebel's devoted followers in carrying on his work during the last half of the nineteenth century. Without their indefatigable efforts, the kindergarten idea may have withered away or at least never have developed in its modern form.

CHAPTER 10

End of Career

TWELVE years after the death of his first wife, Froebel remarried to a woman thirty years his junior. Luise Levin, who had worked at the Keilhau Institute as a kitchen helper and later studied under Froebel, appreciated his genius and returned his affection. His Keilhau associates disapproved of the marriage, considering Luise his social inferior. Nevertheless, the wedding, in July 1851, was a gala affair, promising future happiness for the couple. But serious probleems were only a few weeks ahead.

On August 7, 1851, a crushing blow was dealt Froebel and the kindergarten cause in Germany by a decree issued by Karl von Raumer, Prussian Minister of Education. The governmental edict read, in part:

Whereas it appears by a pamphlet written by Karl Froebel, entitled, *High Schools for Young Ladies and Kindergardens*, that kindergartens form a part of the Froebelian socialistic system, which is calculated to train the youth of the country to atheism, such schools and kindergartens cannot be suffered to exist.[1]

It was ironical that such a sweeping, reactionary order should have come from the hand of von Raumer, one of Pestalozzi's first biographers and a former teacher at Yverdon, who was regarded as one of the most enlightened educators of his time. A detailed account of the event appears in Berthe von Marenholtz-Bülow's *Reminiscences of Friedrich Froebel*. When she first heard the news, the Baroness was incredulous. She writes, "No one was able to find any rational ground for it, and we agreed that there must have been some special exigency, and that it was a mistake of the reactionary measures, that were overstepping all limits at that time."[2]

Even in aristocratic circles the decree created surprise and disapproval. It was assumed that an error had been made, for the idea of prohibiting children's games as dangerous to society seemed too ridiculous to consider. Actually, the confusion had been caused by the belief that Friedrich Froebel and his nephew Karl were one and the same person, or at least represented the same educational philosophy. Karl was busy propagating socialism and atheism, both of which doctrines were completely foreign to Friedrich Froebel's mind.

When Friedrich Froebel heard the news of the ban, he was greatly shocked but took the view that a mistake had been made, that an explanation would straighten out matters and lead to the repeal of the prohibition. Froebel proceeded at once to draft a communication to Minister von Raumer asking him to review the case and to repeal the unjust prohibition. Froebel also sent some of his own writings to Berlin with the letter to indicate the nature of his work.

When a reply came, it was completely unyielding and simply confirmed the Minister's edict: "that he [Froebel] must abide by the prohibition, inasmuch as the principles expressed could not be assented to, and in spite of the confusion of persons, concurrence with that objectionable pamphlet consisted in laying at the foundation of the education of children a highly intricate theory."[3] Despite Froebel's protestation of a deep Christian faith, the Minister asserted that the systems of both Froebels, whatever their differences, were alike in their hostility to Christianity.

"It was clear," wrote the Baroness, "that they would not repeal an ordinance once promulgated, and would not give the cause any examination, but only thrust it aside. Froebel's method did not coincide with the direction of a morbid pietism carried to a great extreme, that prevailed at that time, and the education of the people was considered the most dangerous weapon in the hands of the revolution."[4]

The arbitrary, dogmatic order from the Minister of Education's office came near to being a death blow to Froebel. Never for a moment did he doubt the value of his work, and he was confident of its ultimate triumph. Nevertheless, those were days of severe conflict within his own mind. On one occasion he is quoted by the Baroness as saying, "Now if they will not recognize and support my cause in my native country, I will go to America, where a new life is freely unfolding itself, and a new education of man will find a footing."[5]

In a further effort to obtain a reversal of the edict, Froebel addressed a letter to the King of Prussia. The message was carried to Berlin by the Baroness and delivered to the King in person, but she was pessimistic, writing, "I scarcely felt any confidence, in spite of the King's acceptance of it, in the success of the step. The feeling that prevailed at the court at that time was too much in opposition to the hope expressed by Froebel for the renewal of human society by a correct education corresponding to the actual stage of culture, to lead to the desired result."[6] Indeed, in advocating Froebel's cause, the Baroness herself took the risk of being labeled a radical. Froebel's letter was merely assigned to Minister von Raumer, who was interviewed by the Baroness. She was struck by the Minister's "party fanaticism." His last words to her were, "I shall never allow the establishment of Froebel's kindergartens."[7]

It was of no consequence that many newspaper articles were published defending kindergartens, that there were satirical sketches of the threat to society posed by "three-year-old demagogues," that praise came from places where kindergartens had been founded, and that pedagogical authorities spoke out in their defense. The Minister of Education remained adamant. The Baroness noted "The circumstance, that in many confiscated letters of persons politically compromised, the importance of kindergartens was mentioned as a new foundation for an improved education of the people, was used in official circles to justify the prohibition as a correct one; and this fact may also have served with the King to palliate the error that had occurred."[8]

When she found the Minister immovable, the Baroness asked if the authorities would attempt to prevent families from using Froebel's play materials for their children before sending them to school. Von Raumer conceded that such an action was outside his power. The Baroness recognized this as a loophole, as a means of demonstrating how unjustly the kindergarten cause had been judged; and she reports "a family kindergarten, the first institution of that kind, was opened in the course of that year by our little society in Berlin, and given into the charge of a pupil of Froebel's, Fraülein Erdmann."[9] The Baroness also observed that, though the kindergarten was hindered and to some extent prevented by the government's prohibition, the publicity associated with the ban made the kindergarten idea no longer obscure and helped it to gain importance. A less desirable result was that the cause became the darling of the extreme liberals, making the officials even more suspicious of it and creating the popular misconception of the kindergartens as an irreligious movement. "Thus," remarked the Baroness, "is the cause of the new education more or less associated in the public mind with radicalism, although it has not the least agreement with any radical tendency."[10]

The accusation that Froebel, the most religious of men, found hardest to bear was the charge of atheism. The Hamburg papers began discussing his orthodoxy, and Froebel was deeply distressed to learn that some citizens considered him anti-Christian. But Prussia was only one state. If that state was closed to him and chose to misrepresent and check the kindergarten movement, the rest of Germany was open to Froebel. Before the unification of Germany, when the country was divided into many small and relatively independent principalities, men persecuted by one government could remove themselves to another. Froebel threw himself with redoubled zeal and energy into his work at Marienthal.

Shortly before the Prussian interdiction of the kindergarten, Froebel had sent out invitations to a teachers' meeting to be held at Liebenstein on September 27 - 29, 1851; the principal topics to be discussed, according to Froebel's letter, were kindergarten education, women as teachers and their training for that career, and other contemporary questions on education that might be suggested in the course of the meeting.[11] Despite the ministerial decree banning the kindergarten, plans for the conference proceeded. The Baroness von Marenholtz-Bülow commented that persecution by the reactionaries "gave only greater importance to the coming investigation of the Froebelian method by specialists, and Froebel entertained the hope of again seeing his idea brought publicly into estimation through favorable judgments of it."[12]

The convention opened on the morning of September 27 in the hall of the Liebenstein Baths and its deliberations were marked by great harmony. One of its important results was adoption of a "Declaration" by the assembled educators stating that they considered Froebel's system to be "far removed from all partisanship and every one-sided tendency; that it must be looked upon as a deeper foundation of both theoretical and practical education; that it promised essentially to advance school culture; and that it had proved itself particularly fitted to improve family education through the culture of women for their educational calling, which it involved."[13] The group also sponsored the beginning of a new periodical, entitled A Journal for Promoting the Endeavors of Friedrich Froebel for the Accomplishment of the Education of Man According to the Principle of Unfolding Development with the Aim of Achieving a General Harmony of Life, under the editorship of Bruno Marquart in Dresden.

Among the influential signers of the Declaration was a well-known educator Friedrich Adolf Wilhelm Diesterweg, who was extraordinarily active in addressing teachers' meetings, in organizing teachers' associations, and in publishing magazines and textbooks written according to Pestalozzi's principle of self-activity—all of which contributed to the rise of the teaching profession.

During the winter and early spring after the Liebenstein conference, Froebel's health began to fail. On April 21, 1852, a seventieth birthday celebration in his honor was held by his students. The occasion gave Froebel great pleasure. The students dressed in symbolic costumes, the Salzung and Liebenstein kindergarten children played games for him, and letters and presents came from kindergarten teachers working in different places, expressing grateful affection for the master.

After this festival, Froebel's life appeared happier and more tranquil than usual; but he continued to be disturbed by news of controversies which came to him concerning his ideas, and his health further deteriorated. Even so, in April, 1852, he accepted an invitation to participate in a teachers' convention, meeting in Gotha. According to Middendorff's account, Froebel entered the convention hall during Diesterweg's address; and on his arrival the assembly rose as one man. At the end of the speech he was further welcomed by three cheers proposed by the president of the conference. Froebel's contribution to the program concerned the teaching of natural sciences to the young, and he gave examples of his method and its results. Demonstrations of kindergarten lessons were also arranged. In the discussions which followed, Froebel dwelt on the important influence the kindergarten movement must have on the position of women and also on the necessity of giving every teacher of young children a knowledge of the kindergarten system.

The Baroness von Marenholtz-Bülow, in her *Reminiscences of Friedrich Froebel* adds further information on the kindergarten ban, eight years after Froebel's death: "In 1860 there was a public abrogation of the prohibition of the innocent kindergarten, but the mistrust roused against it in many quarters has never been entirely removed. The repeal was to me a greater satisfaction because my unremitting endeavors, particularly with the minister of the 'new era,' had helped to bring it about."[14]

CHAPTER 11

Spread of Froebel's Ideas

THOUGH the suppression of public kindergartens in Germany by reactionary government officials was a severe blow to Froebel in his last years, in the long run it probably benefited the kindergarten movement. The ban in Germany led to a widespread emigration of liberal-minded Germans to America and Western European countries. In many cases, notably in England and the United States, the children of such emigrants became pupils in newly established kindergartens, helping to disseminate Froebel's ideas.

In the years following Froebel's death, the most effective propagandist for the "New Education" was the Baroness Berthe von Marenholtz-Bülow, whose activities have been previously described. Her tireless advocacy of kindergarten principles in England, France, Belgium, Holland, Italy, and Switzerland, as well as in her native Germany, was a major factor in spreading Froebel's fame and his educational philosophy. The efforts of the Countess were also chiefly responsible for removing the ban on kindergartens in Prussia, in 1860, eight years after Froebel's death. Students trained by the Countess carried the movement to Finland, Russia, and elsewhere.

The Austrian government was the first to accept the kindergarten as an essential unit in the national educational scheme. Inspired first by the German philosopher Fichte and afterward by the Baroness von Marenholtz during her stay at Liebenstein, a kindergarten normal school was established in 1872 at Huffstein. As a general rule, however, the kindergarten idea did not receive adoption or endorsement by governments. Instead, its early dissemination came mainly through the voluntary work of dedicated individuals and special societies throughout Europe. Before the end of the nineteenth century, instruction in Froebelian principles was usually required in most normal and teacher-training institutions in Europe. Occasionally the kindergarten was combined with the infant school movement, and some of its original characteristics were thereby changed.

The kindergarten movement lost two leading advocates in 1871 with the deaths of Thekla Naveau and Wilhelmine Marquart. Frau Naveau had been a pupil of Middendorff's and was the author of *Stories for the Home and the Kindergarten*. Frau Marquart had studied with Froebel and conducted a kindergarten in connection with her husband's school at Dresden. She was responsible for training many excellent kindergarten teachers.

Another active worker in the cause was Heinrich August Koehler of Gotha, who was converted to Froebel's ideas at the Gotha conference of 1852, and thereafter became one of the best-known exponents in Europe of the Froebel system. Koehler began with a private class for the education of his own children and shortly thereafter became the head of a training school for kindergarten teachers. He was invited by the Russian government to represent the kindergarten movement at the celebration of Peter the Great's two-hundredth anniversary, and also at the Polytechnic Exhibition at Moscow in 1873. Koehler was one of the editors of a journal, *Kindergarten and Elementary Classes*, the official organ of the German Froebel Association.

Institutions, such as the Pestalozzi-Froebel House in Berlin, established by Froebel's grandniece in 1881, became influential centers for the spread of creative ideas on elementary education. The grandniece, Henrietta Schrader, had spent the summer of 1848 at Keilhau. During the following winter, she studied with Froebel at Dresden, afterward kept house for him, and helped teach the children while he lived in the farmhouse at Liebenstein. Later she returned home and became a teacher in her native village. Shortly before Froebel's death, she came back to Liebenstein and was a member of the last training class that Froebel ever taught. Her career thereafter was varied: she maintained a kindergarten in connection with her school at Watzun; in 1863 - 64 she went to Geneva to set up the Jardin d'Enfants; and some years later she married, moved to Berlin, and continued her educational efforts.

It is an ironical fact that only in Germany, where the kindergarten system originated, was the idea handicapped by governmental regulations for a period of years. Concerning this situation, Frank P. Graves in his *Great Educators of Three Centuries* (1912) commented:

The deadening effects of the ministerial decree, despite the efforts of the heroic baroness [Berthe von Marenholtz-Bülow] in establishing and encouraging kindergarten associations, hung over the German states for a decade; and even since the removal of the ban, kindergartens have, with few exceptions, never been recognized as real schools or part of the regular state system. The kindergartners are not subject to the requirements demanded of all other elementary teachers, and are forbidden to touch on the formal school subjects or work of any sort that would seen to duplicate the primary curriculum. Even to-day [1911] the German kindergarten is regarded as little more than a day nursery or convenient place to deposit small children and have them amused. The educational principles for which Froebel contended are not generally conceded in Germany.[1]

I *Kindergarten in England*

The work entitled *Friedrich Froebel and English Education*, by a number of authors and edited by Evelyn Lawrence, traces in detail the history of the Froebel movement in England. For various reasons the British Isles proved fertile soil for the kindergarten idea. Among the reasons cited are the existence of infant schools for more than fifty years; the legislation which kept younger children from being employed in factories, necessitating provision for their care while older members of the family were at work; and the desire among religious-minded persons for institutions to teach religion and morals.

As previously noted, the cotton mill owner Robert Owen established schools, between 1816 and 1824, where young children were encouraged to sing and to dance, to take an interest in natural objects, and to understand passages read to them before they had learned to read. Owen's infant schools inspired the opening of similar schools in London and elsewhere. The later schools, however, showed little understanding of child nature. Moral instruction became the predominant feature, free movement was discouraged, and the infants were required to sit quietly for all oral lessons.

In 1837 the Home and Colonial Society was founded in England for the purpose of training teachers, especially teachers in infant schools, according to Pestalozzian principles. Pestalozzi himself had believed that infants are best taught at home by their mothers, but some of his English adherents wanted to adapt his ideas to more formal instruction.

In any event, the concept of different methods for teaching very young and older children was well established and accepted in England and thus paved the way for ready reception of the "New Education" or kindergarten principles. An important element, too, was a great increase in the number of liberal-minded German residents, in London and other main centers, who emigrated to Britain and America after the failure of the 1848 revolution in Germany. Among the most influential were Bertha and Johannes Ronge, who came to London in 1851 to begin a kindergarten. Bertha Ronge had been one of Froebel's pupils in Hamburg in 1849, and the Ronges had founded kindergartens in Germany prior to their London sojourn. Highly important too was the visit, previously noted, of the Baroness von Marenholtz-Bülow to England in 1854.

Articles on the kindergarten were printed in such leading newspapers as *The Times* and the *Athenaeum.* Charles Dickens met the Baroness and visited the Ronges' kindergarten, after which he wrote a well-informed account for his periodical *Household Words.* Public attitudes were also influenced by Dickens' novels portraying sympathetically the plight of children, especially in the lower levels of society.

Aid in spreading the kindergarten message came through an educational exhibition sponsored by the Society of Arts in St. Martin's Hall, London, opened by the Prince Consort in 1854. A display of Froebel's gifts and occupations was demonstrated by Heinrich Hoffman, another of Froebel's pupils and head of the training institution in Hamburg. Among the visitors was Henry Barnard, the American educator. Hoffman remained in England, after the exhibition closed, to train teachers. The Ronges also undertook the preparation of teachers in their school. As a result, the kindergarten movement began to spread to Manchester, Leeds, and other communities. Hoffman returned to Germany for a time but then was recalled to England by the Home and Colonial Society to direct student studies in two schools—one for infant school teachers in government-aided schools and the other for the instruction of nursery governesses and teachers in higher class schools. Hoffman was responsible for the training of kindergarten teachers in the non-government section. At the same time, a school was opened for practice and demonstration.

In 1893, the Home and Colonial Society became the National Froebel Union for examination and certification purposes for non-government students. The society also performed a useful service in offering evening classes in kindergarten methods for infant school teachers. The kindergarten movement had become sufficiently important by now to inspire the establishment of societies, including the London Froebel Society and the Manchester Froebel Society. These organizations had dual purposes: promotion of the kindergarten idea and assurance of a supply of properly qualified teachers who would understand the principles of the kindergarten. Curiously, there was a shortage of literature on the kindergarten in Britain. Educators in England, for that reason, found valuable such American publications as Elizabeth Peabody's magazine, *The Kindergarten Teacher;* Mrs. Horace Mann's translation of *Reminiscences of Friedrich Froebel,* by the Baroness Berthe von Marenholtz-Bülow; and Henry Barnard's eight hundred-page compilation, *Kindergarten and Child Culture,* which remained a treasure of information for kindergartners during the early years of the movement.

The best of the English kindergartens seemed to have followed closely Froebel's teachings. As recalled by a pupil at Croydon, for example, the boys and girls enrolled were between six and seven years of age, the morning sessions opened with prayers and a formal march around the room, followed by the kindergarten games and occupations.

After 1875, the English association adopted the title of the Froebel Society for the Promotion of the Kindergarten System. It undertook to sponsor a series of lectures for children's nurses and set up a committee to examine prospective kindergarten teachers. The final examination upon which the certificate of the Society was to be granted was comprehensive over a wide range of subjects:

reading, writing, arithmetic, grammar, geography, history, English literature, theory and history of education, physical education, Froebel's writings, geometry, stories, poetry, gymnastics, singing, physiology, physics, zoology, botany, geology, hygiene, kindergarten occupations, and practical lessons given by the students.

One of the first presidents of the Froebel Society was Emily Shirreff, who had written a number of aticles for the *Education Journal* on kindergarten matters, followed by several excellent books: *Principles of the Kindergarten* (1876), *Sketch of Froebel's Life* (1877), *The Kindergarten at Home* (1882), and *Moral Training* (1892).

The two special concerns of the Froebel Society, as noted, were to assure an adequate number of kindergarten teachers and the inspection and registration of kindergartens. Safeguards were needed to prevent teachers who knew nothing of the principles of kindergarten education from adopting some of the songs, games, gifts, and occupations and calling their schools kindergartens. The work of inspecting kindergartens and placing approved institutions on a graded list was carefully planned, using well-qualified inspectors, who were provided with directions for applying specific points in judging the schools.

Keen understanding of Froebel's doctrines is shown by a paper "What Froebel Did for Young Children," read by a Miss Manning at a London conference in 1884:

The teaching is not direct instruction. It trains the senses and the observing powers through handling and doing; it exercises the muscles and limbs, it takes advantage of the imitative faculty, it appeals to the fancy by means of stories and talks, it works through the affections, it draws forth helpfulness and self-respect. The kindergarten ought to be open for the instruction of young girls, nurses and nursemaids, where they might learn how to treat and how to train the children, to young mothers and to all who have charge of little children.[2]

As time passed, it was recognized that the formal examinations for kindergarten teachers in training were overloaded with academic and practical subjects, making it difficult for students to complete the course. Beginning in 1884, therefore, it was decided that there should be two examinations and two types of certificates.

The first, the Lower or Elementary Certificate for assistant kindergarten and governesses and a Higher Certificate for the heads of kindergartens. Even the Lower Certificate examination demanded rather broad preparation for the student. Students were expected to know something of the lives of Pestalozzi and Froebel and their works and teaching; principles of education as taught by Pestalozzi and Froebel and their application to the teaching of elementary subjects; familiar plants and animals and the ordinary phenomena of nature; practical knowledge of Froebel's "occupations"; and ability to sing songs connected with the games. On the practical side, candidates were required to tell a story, conduct a game, give a lesson on one of the occupations, teach a lesson on an elementary school subject, and conduct some simple gymnastic exercises. Requirements for granting the Higher Certificate were considerably stiffer at every step. Doubtless because of these rigorous examinations, the growth of the kindergarten movement was slowed. Only a small number of students volunteered for training, and the educational level of those who did apply was low.

English kindergartens as they developed in the nineteenth century deviated in at least one respect from Froebel's principles. More emphasis was placed on games organized by teachers than on the children's own free play. The teachers' justification was that games devised by them would more effectively serve the kindergarten's goals of intellectual training, ethical teaching, physical exercise, dramatic action, musical and rhythmical training, and the use of simple, concise, and accurate language than the unorganized, perhaps aimless, pupils' play. Some Froebel games were introduced, but teachers and students were encouraged to invent new games. Gradually, traditional English nursery rhymes replaced Froebel's German singing games.

The success of the English kindergartens and their favorable reception in educational circles aroused interest elsewhere in the British Empire. Before the end of the nineteenth century there were active kindergarten movements in Australia, Canada, Cape Colony, India, and New Zealand. In fact, the kindergarten had become a worldwide phenomenon. A writer in the *Pratt Institute Monthly*, November 1895, stated: "When not recognized by the government of a country, kindergartens have often been introduced through Christian missions. Missionaries find the kindergarten most helpful in reaching the children and through them the homes of those whom they wish to benefit. In a letter from China we are told that Froebel's method must be valuable, as it is so entirely the opposite of the artificial methods of the Chinese. In Japan, in India, in the Sandwich Islands, in Austria, in Turkey, in Russia, France, Switzerland, Norway and Sweden, the kindergarten has found a home."[3]

II *Kindergarten in America*

The kindergarten idea caught on quickly in the United States. Within four years after Froebel's death, one of his students had set up a kindergarten in Wisconsin; within eight years an American woman inspired by his work had organized a kindergarten in Boston; twelve years later one of Luise Froebel's students had established a kindergarten in New York City; and in 1873 the first public school kindergarten opened in St. Louis.

It has been stated that the influence of the kindergarten has been more marked in the United States than in any other country. When Henry Barnard, American educational leader, returned home in 1854, after having been a delegate to an educational exhibition in London and having seen a kindergarten demonstration there, he wrote at length and enthusiastically about the movement. His writings inspired Elizabeth Palmer Peabody, in 1860, to open a kindergarten in Boston, though she lacked firsthand training or experience in the field. The institution was immediately successful and the children enrolled highly responsive. Miss Peabody was not fully satisfied with her efforts, however, feeling that she needed to know more about kindergarten principles and the spirit of Froebel's work. She therefore proceeded to tour European kindergartens in 1867 - 68, visited the Baroness von Marenholtz-Bülow, and studied with Froebel's widow, who had been settled in Hamburg for several years.

After Miss Peabody came back to the United States, she corrected the errors in her kindergarten program. Together with her sister, Mary (Peabody) Mann, Horace Mann's widow, she was instrumental in furthering the cause by writing, lecturing, starting a periodical to explain and spread Froebel's ideas, translating basic kindergarten works from the German, and forming a Froebel Union. The remainder of Miss Peabody's life was spent in interesting parents, philanthropists, and school boards in the kindergarten movement. In many respects, she was the American counterpart of the Baroness von Marenholtz-Bülow in Europe.

Two other pioneers were Matilda H. Kriege and her daughter Alma Kriege, who started a kindergarten department in a German school in New York, later transferred to Boston. Both teachers had received their training from the Baroness in Berlin, and the mother had been a personal friend of Froebel's. The Krieges had brought with them from Germany a certain amount of kindergarten material, imported additional items, and persuaded dealers in school supplies to begin manufacturing similar gift and occupation material. Matilda translated into English the Baroness von Marenholtz-Bülow's *The Child, Its Nature and Relations; an Elucidation of Froebel's Principles of Education* (N.Y., 1877).

A principal proponent of the kindergarten in America, as previously mentioned, was Henry Barnard, secretary of the Connecticut Board of Education and editor for many years of the *American Journal of Education*. His article "Froebel's System of Infant Gardens" contained the first mention of the kindergarten to appear in an American periodical. Later, as the first U.S. Commissioner of Education, Barnard recommended to Congress the establishment of a system of public schools for the District of Columbia, to include kindergartens. His monumental work, *Kindergarten and Child Culture*, issued in 1881, has remained a primary source of information on the early stages of the subject.

St. Louis was among the earliest American communities to initiate a kindergarten. In 1872, Susan E. Blow petitioned the school board for a room in which to undertake the first local experiment. Giving her services without salary, she opened and continued to operate a training school for the next twelve years. This institution stimulated the growth of public kindergartens, the first of which became a part of the St. Louis educational system in 1873. Within a decade, there were more than fifty public kindergartens, enrolling about eight thousand pupils, in St. Louis. The St. Louis superintendent of schools, subsequently U.S. Commissioner of Education, William T. Harris, strongly supported the development. Miss Blow was a translator of *The Mottoes and Commentaries of Friedrich*

Froebel's Mother Play (N.Y., 1895), and the author of several informative works on kindergarten education.

Kindergartens received early impetus in New York from Felix Adler and Heber Newton, whose aim was to bring the children of the working class under the kindegarten influence. Adler established a free kindergarten in 1878, an institution later expanded to a full curriculum for children up to age fourteen. Newton, a minister, in the same year opened the first mission kindergarten, connected with his church. When Columbia University's Teachers College began instruction in 1887, the kindergarten was made a basic feature of its work.

A Chicago Froebel Association was formed in the 1870's. A distinctive aspect of the Chicago plan was its connection with Jane Addams' Hull House. Miss Addams and her associate Ellen Gates Starr were emulating the work which they had seen in operation at Toynbee Hall in London, reputed to be the world's first social settlement.

The movement soon spread to the West Coast. Emma Marwedel, a pioneer kindergarten teacher, who was invited to California in 1876 by the Froebel Union, established successful training classes in Los Angeles, Oakland, and Berkeley. The "Golden Gate Association" in San Francisco at one time supported forty-one free kindergartens and a training school for teachers.

Thus, well before the turn of the century, the kindergarten concept was solidly established, popularly accepted, and widely disseminated in the United States.

The status of Froebel's ideas and of kindergartens in the twentieth-century educational world will be reviewed in the next chapter.

CHAPTER 12

Froebel in the Twentieth Century

ON the basis of more than a century of practical experience and extensive research in education and psychology since Friedrich Froebel's death in 1852, vastly more is known today about these fields than in his day. Various writers have attempted a reexamination and reevaluation of the Froebelian theories in the light of later findings. Examples are F. A. Cavanagh's "The Place of Froebel in Modern Education,"[1] J. P. Slight's "Froebel and the English Primary School of Today,"[2] and Barbara Priestman's *Froebel Education To-day*.[3] Two older, highly perceptive studies, are William H. Kilpatrick's *Froebel's Kindergarten Principles Critically Examined*[4] and Graham Wallas' "A Criticism of Froebelian Pedagogy."[5]

Twentieth-century educators apparently are in general agreement that much of Froebel's thought is outmoded and perhaps even discredited. In fact, because of obscurity of expression, a great deal of it has never been fully understood by kindergarten teachers. On the other hand, the value of Froebel's long, careful sympathetic study of children remains of inestimable importance, for it opened a new world in childhood education.

Graham Wallas begins his critical essay "by expressing my personal gratitude for the main result of Froebel's long and self-sacrificing life. I thank him for having done so much to introduce happiness, activity and love into our schools for young children; but especially I would thank him for having helped to bring the science of education into closer relation with the science of life."[6] Wallas then proceeded to offer severe strictures on specific aspects of Froebel's method: e.g., a minimizing of human tradition as a formative influence; neglect of the training of attention, habits, and character; ignoring the distinction between work, and play as a relief after work; postponing too long the learning of such arts as reading and writing; misunderstanding of the conditions under which students gain knowledge; and delay in introducing the child to real music, real literature, real art, and other great forms of human achievement. Wallas charged also that Froebel exaggerated and oversimplified the various stages of a child's development, he sentimentalized, wrote poor verse, and was too much of a symbolist.

The question then remains: Can Froebel's practice be separated from his theories? He himself would have strongly objected to any separation; and he was critical of Pestalozzi for the latter's failure to base his practice on theory, commenting, "That Pestalozzi himself was carried away and bewildered by this great intellectual machine of his appears from the fact that he could never give any definite account of his idea, his plan, his intention."[7] Nevertheless, a division between practice and theory in Froebel's case is possible and desirable.

After examining and dismissing as unproven and unscientific a number of Froebel's principles, Kilpatrick asks "how a system such as we have just rejected would have made so great a stir in the world."[8] Kilpatrick suggests that many Froebel adherents have known too little of other educational thought, have given Froebel personal credit for what in reality grew out of the spirit of the age, and furthermore have ascribed to him all subsequent progress in kindergarten and childhood education.

But Kilpatrick finds quite sufficient justification for Froebel's fame. Among the strong features of the Froebel system, as viewed by Kilpatrick, are his love for and sympathy with children, respect for the individuality of the child, his rejection of the doctrine of total depravity, recognition of the educational value of play, and cultivation of the child's natural interests through encouragement of initiative and self-activity. Also fundamental was Froebel's insistence upon social relationship; he was convinced that the child has a natural inclination to social intercourse. The family is the first social group known to the child, following which, Froebel held, it is the duty of the kindergarten and school to provide opportunities for the child to develop socially through active participation in social life. Froebel was a pioneer, too, in introducing esthetic elements into the kindergarten program long before primary schools in general had recognized their place in early education. Also, his interest in nature study and school gardens was far ahead of his time. To become truly educated, Froebel asserted, the senses, especially hearing and vision, must be cultivated; for children may become indifferent because they are never aware of the beauties around them and because they do not play creatively.

For Froebel, education was closely linked with nature, a reflection of his great love for the outdoors. He viewed nature as complete, as a single system, and maintained that education should likewise be a whole, inclusive of all the child's activities. Everything was likened to nature. The growth of weak saplings in the forest to full-grown trees, for example, is compared to development of the child from infancy to maturity. The teacher's responsibility is to guide the child's growth, especially to cultivate the abilities already existing in him.

John Dewey, whose own educational philosophy was profoundly influenced by Froebel's ideas, both praises and criticizes certain of the latter's basic concepts:

Froebel's recognition of the significance of the native capacities of children, his loving attention to them, and his influence in inducing others to study them, represent perhaps the most effective single force in modern educational theory in effecting widespread acknowledgment of the idea of growth. But his formulation of the notion of development and his organization of devices for promoting it were badly hampered by the fact that he conceived development to be the unfolding of a ready-made latent principle. He failed to see that growing is growth, developing is development, and consequently placed the emphasis upon the completed product. Thus he set up a goal which meant the arrest of growth, and a criterion which is not applicable to immediate guidance of powers, save through translation into abstract and symbolic formulae.[9]

Like Froebel, Dewey had no patience with the traditional system of making children sit quietly in orderly rows. He believed that a good teacher should be able to direct the natural interests of children in such a manner that they would grow mentally and socially, as well as physically. In the spirit of Froebel, Dewey and his followers agreed that children should be permitted to move about in the classroom, learn with their hands as well as with their minds, associate freely with their companions, and thus live in a normal school society.

Among the early critics of Froebel's system were Stanley Hall and other leaders of the Child Study Association. The critics condemned such Froebel "occupations" as pricking and sewing, pea and stick work, threading of small beads, and similar activities involving manipulation with the fingers, paper folding and drawing on lines with a pencil—presumably because of eye strain. For such work, they substituted brushwork and free drawing. Free play, in which the children took the lead, while the teacher remained in the background, replaced organized kindergarten games; and the "Mother Songs" were superseded by songs relevant to the child's own life and capable of being dramatized.

The abandonment of traditional kindergarten practices was viewed with strong disapproval by orthodox Froebel devotees. The split between the old and new interpretations of Froebel's teaching was most controversial in the United States but extended in a milder form to England. Concerning reactions in the latter country, P. Woodham-Smith, tracing the history of the Froebel movement in England, notes that "the change to the newer and freer methods of interpretation was welcomed by the majority of kindergartens within a comparatively short time, while the gradual amancipation from gifts, occupations and set drawings in favor of educational handiwork in the syllabus of the National Froebel Union brought relief to those training to become kindergarten teachers, and gave scope to those of them who had artistic gifts."[10]

John Dewey, whose practices and teaching paralleled Froebel's in many respects, as noted, defends the use of play as a learning device. In his *Democracy and Education* he observes, "Doubtless the fact that children normally engage in play and work out of school has seemed to many educators a reason why they should concern themselves in school with things radically different. School time seemed too precious to spend in doing over again what chldren were sure to do any way."[11] But, Dewey points out, play can produce an important educational by-product. Mental and moral growth are facilitated, he states, if the school sets up a proper environment of work and play.

Following in the tradition of Froebel's "gifts and occupations," Dewey lists types of activities which have found their way into schools: work with paper, cardboard, wood, leather, cloth, yarns, clay and sand, and metals, with or without tools; such processes as folding, cutting, pricking, measuring, molding, modeling, pattern-making, heating and cooling, and the use of the hammer, saw, file, and other tools; also outdoor excursions, gardening, cooking, sewing, printing, bookbinding, weaving, painting, drawing, singing, dramatization, story-telling, reading and writing, and a countless variety of plays and games.[12] It is not enough, however, as Dewey points out, to introduce plays and games, handwork and manual exercises into the classroom. The aim of such activities should be to generate intellectual results and encourage socialized dispositions as well as manual skills and technical efficiency.

The socialized Dewey school, based upon Dewey's philosophy of education, became widely known at home and abroad. A scheme based on Froebel's principle of self-activity and unity, to extend throughout the elementary grades, was worked out by Dewey and his associates. The first aim of the kindergarten teacher, it was held, should be the creation of a community. Along with Froebel, it was believed that a child lives in his play, and if suitably directed derives many benefits from play activities. As children grow older they are introduced to the world around them, such as the farm and the house, handwork, simple carpentry, weaving and pottery, in accordance with their interests.

Shortly prior to World War I, a rival system, known as the "Montessori Method," chiefly for teaching kindergarten and primary-grade children, was designed by an Italian physician and educator, Maria Montessori. Although analogous in various features to Froebel's principles, the founder was unwilling to concede that her system had any connection with Froebel's teaching. The Montessori method was planned to develop the child's own natural desire to learn and to perform well. An important aspect of the plan is the use of special teaching materials designed to develop the child's sensory and muscular responses. Some of these devices closely resemble Froebel's gifts and occupations. For example, pieces of cardboard with large raised letters on sandpaper surfaces are given the child to feel and copy, from which he learns to read and write; geography may be taught by large jigsaw puzzles of the seas and continents, cut along natural boundaries; cutouts of geometrical figures are given the child to fit together; and arithmetic may be taught by working with beads strung on wires. Two Montessori principles that continue to influence modern education are respect for the child's individuality and encouragement of his personal freedom—concepts with which Froebel would have been in complete sympathy. The Montessori method had a widespread vogue in Europe and America for a period of years and did much to call attention to the importance of the early stages of education. During the 1960's there was an enormous revival of interest in the Montessori method. By the end of the 1960's, more than five hundred private schools in the United States had been organized on Montessori principles.

In her short study *Froebel Education To-day*, Barbara Priestman analyzes differences between Froebel schools and others, as they operate currently. She concludes that a modern Froebel school will consider the child's environment of first importance. The atmosphere is one of friendliness, mutual respect, and of love without false sentiment. Preferably rooms will be sunny with low windows opening on some pleasant scene. Flower arrangements and good pictures add to the attractiveness of the environment. In a Froebel school, Miss Priestman notes, teachers and parents work closely together to bring about an intimate understanding between school and home. Parents are given an opportunity to learn how their children are being educated and teachers have a chance to know the parents' point of view.

In a typical Froebel kindergarten class, as described by Miss Priestman, one group of children may be playing families with a tea set and a house made by an arrangement of tables and chairs; several boys will be using hammer, saws, and nails to construct a boat or an airplane; other children are arranging flowers, painting at easels, or doing arithmetic sums. The teacher remains in the background, perhaps listening to children display their reading ability, but always available when needed. It is the business of the teacher to watch and stimulate activity, not to impose ready-made plans on the children. As O. B. Priestman states, "A sensitive teacher is able to find the way the interests of her class are going, and to foster by the material she provides, or the suggestions she makes, those interests which seem likely to be most productive."[13]

Summing up the place of Froebel in modern education, F. A. Cavanagh maintains that "although we must discard that part of Froebel's philosophy which depended on his own peculiarities or on his age, yet there remains a spirit which is alive and active. Froebel himself had no static conception of his system: indeed he remarked once that it would take 300 years to work out. . . . This living spirit of Froebel is seen not only in details such as the value now attached to handwork, nature study, gardens, etc., but also in certain features of modern educational theory that reflect at least some of his views."[14]

Cavanagh identifies four such features as of first significance: (1) the importance of early education, and the value of each stage for itself; (2) the need for child psychology—though Froebel's own psychology was weak, he paved the way for modern child study and for scientific psychology; (3) the value of play, especially as developed into free play with toys and other material; and (4) the belief that every child merits respect and treatment as an individual.[15]

The years between World Wars I and II saw a great development in the study of child psychology both in Europe and America. The findings have influenced schools in the direction of greater attention to the individual needs of children and the ages at which they should begin to learn such skills as reading and writing.

An English educator, P. Woodham-Smith concludes: "Perhaps enough has been written to show that there is a very direct connection between the work and ideas of Froebel more than a hundred years ago and the modern or progressive attitude towards children and their education; and that the debt of all who have any love or understanding of children and their needs to Froebel and his followers is incalculable."[16]

A piece of evidence to demonstrate the international spread of the kindergarten idea is cited by Robert G. Kaiser in his recent work, *Russia, the People and the Power*. Kaiser writes, "Kindergartens for four-to-six-year olds . . . care for about two-thirds of all the children in the country [the Soviet Union] in that age group. The curriculum—provided from Moscow in a handbook for teachers—calls for singing, dancing, drawing, memorizing and some reading, all in groups. The best kindergartens are happy refuges of laughter and fun, but many don't live up to the ideal."[17] Froebel certainly would have approved the spirit which Kaiser observed as prevailing in the "best kindergartens."

The judgment of another modern educator is relevant to an evaluation of Friedrich Froebel's place in twentieth-century education. Robert Ulich of Harvard University, in his *History of Educational Thought*, writes:

Though for the layman Froebel's name is connected with the kindergarten, he is also one of the great inspirers of modern progressive education in a more general sense. The judgment one passes on his philosophical premises will depend on one's sympathy with Froebel's Christian form of pantheism. Certainly this metaphysics allows for much romantic speculation about the nature of God and man; it exposes itself to philosophical criticism, like any other metaphysical system of thought; and it has sometimes degenerated into mere sentimentality among followers of Froebel, who did not possess his power of synthesis. On the other hand, Froebel's influence may convince us that it is not empirical exactness alone but profoundness of intuition and depth of faith which give ever-new inspiration to mankind in its struggle for a better life.[18]

Froebel's Gifts and Occupations

Gift I
Box of six worsted balls of 1½-inch diameter, red, yellow, blue, orange, green, violet.

Gift II
Box containing a cube, a cylinder and a ball of 1½-inch diameter, with suspending frame.

Gift III
Box containing a two-inch cube, divided once in every direction, forming eight small cubes of one inch.

Gift IV
Box containing a two-inch cube, divided into eight solid oblongs, two inches by one inch by one half inch.

Gift V
Box containing a three-inch cube, divided twice in each direction, forming twenty-seven one-inch cubes, three of which are divided into halves, and three into quarters.

Gift VI
Box containing a three-inch cube, divided to form twenty-seven solid oblongs, of which three are divided into halves to form four-sided prisms, and six into halves to form square half-cubes.

Occupations
1 Tablet laying. Square and triangular planes of polished wood of two colors, for constructing designs.
2 Paper folding. Four-inch squares and hexagons of assorted colors, also larger sheets of white and colored paper.
3 Paper cutting. Material as above.

4 Paper plaiting or weaving. Colored paper in the form of strips, and bases for interweaving.

5 Paper twisting. Paper and cardboard strips of different widths.

6 Stick plaiting. Smooth and flexible strips of wood ten inches long.

7 Stick laying. Round and quadrangular sticks twelve inches long.

8 Pea work. Small pointed sticks for joining together soaked and softened peas, to form skeleton three-dimensional constructions.

9 Wood and cork work. Corks, pointed sticks, and wires.

10 Ring laying. Metal rings of different sizes and segments of these.

11 Thread laying. Twelve- and eighteen-inch soft cotton threads to be used as lines to form curved designs.

12 Drawing. Checkered paper and books.

13 Pricking. White and colored cardboard and paper, checkered paper; pricking needle with handle.

14 Sewing. Colored wools, silks and cottons. Perforated cards with pictures, patterns, letters, maps, etc. Cardboard objects to be decorated with embroidery, etc.

MISCELLANEOUS. Painting, drawing, clay modelling, sand modelling, ravelling bunting, bead threading, Japanese straw-work, basketry, cane weaving, stencilling.

The above particulars are summarized from the publisher's catalogue in Mary Gurney's "Kindergarten Practice," 1877.

From: Lawrence, Evelyn, ed. *Friedrich Froebel and English Education.* N.Y.: Philosophical Library, 1953, pp. 238 - 39.

Syllabus of
Froebel's Education of Man

1. Education defined by the law of divine unity.
2. The knowledge to which education should lead man.
3. Free self-activity the essential method in education.
4. The relations existing between teacher and pupil conditioned upon the law of right, not upon despotic authority.
5. Unity, individuality, and diversity the phases of human development.
6. Self-control to be fostered from infancy, and willfulness to be guarded against.
7. The earliest religious influence in the development of child nature.
8. The several stages of childhood, boyhood, and manhood to be duly respected in their order.
9. The various powers of the human being to be developed by means of suitable external work.
10. A parallelism between the development of the individual and that of the race.
11. Process and order of the development of the senses.
12. Line of separation between infancy and childhood.
13. Nature and value of the child's play.
14. Importance of due attention to matters of food and clothing.
15. The aim of parental care is to arouse to full activity all the child's physical and mental powers.
16. The child's early efforts at investigation of properties.
17. Value of the early attempts at drawing.
18. Early knowledge gained from association with the older members of the family.
19. Line of separation between childhood and boyhood.
20. Boyhood is the period for learning on the child's part; for training on the part of parent and teacher.
21. To strengthen and direct the will is the essential work of the school.
22. The true basis of right will culture lies in the proper activity and firmness of the feelings and of the heart.

23. The family is the type of true life and the source of active interest in all surroundings.

24. Importance of wisely nurturing the formative instinct as manifested in the child's efforts to assist in work.

25. The early adventures of the boy are in quest of knowledge, and they result in parallel development of power.

26. The games of boyhood educate for life by awakening and cultivating many civil and moral virtues.

27. The love of story and of song are further manifestations of right mental activity and should be utilized to the child's development in knowledge and power.

28. The evil characteristics so often manifested in boy-life have been developed by neglect of right tendencies and by arbitrary and willful interference with right activities.

29. The true remedy for any evil is to find the original good quality that has been repressed or misled and then to foster and guide it aright.

30. Much harm is done by attributing wrong motives to deeds that were mere results of impulse without any due appreciation of consequences.

31. The purpose of the school and of its work is to give to the child the inner relations and meanings of what was before merely external and unrelated.

32. However inefficient the teacher may be, the child naturally comes to him with a spirit of faith and hope.

33. The intensive power decreases and the extensive power increases in passing from youth to old age.

34. Errors in dealing with these powers result in serious and permanent harm.

35. The essential work of the school is to associate facts into principles, not to teach isolated facts.

36. The personality and the surroundings of the child constitute the essential subjects of school instruction.

37. Religion defined in respect to three distinct and harmonious phases.

38. Religious instruction must assume the preexistence of some degree of religion as its basis of reception and influence.

39. The unity of God and man is illustrated and demonstrated in the observation and experience of man in his personal relations.

40. Only so far as we comprehend the spiritual in human relations, and live in accord therewith, can we attain to full conception of the relations between God and man.

41. The purpose of all existence in the world of nature is the revelation of God.

42. In the development of the inner life of the individual man the history of the spiritual development of the race is repeated.

43. Parents and teachers should lead children into familiarity with nature and into recognition of God in nature.

44. Active force is the ultimate cause of every phenomenon in nature.

45. Matter and force mutually condition each other, so that it is impossible to think of one without the other.

46. The sphere is the outward manifestation of unimpeded force diffusing itself freely and equally in all directions.

47. The crystal represents the action of force unequally or in different directions.

48. The various crystalline forms may be traced in necessary order of development from the simplest to the most complex.

49. The relations of life forms to crystalline forms.

50. Relations of the number five in plant forms to the numbers two and three.

51. Manifestations in the diversity and progressive changes of plant forms of the peculiar nature of the inner living force.

52. Illustration in progressive animal forms of the mutual interrelation of the external and the internal.

53. The law of unity, traced through all manifestations of force, from the simple crystal formation to the spiritual life of man.

54. The essential matter in the study of nature is the observation of objects and their attributes irrespective of any ability to give accepted names.

55. The contemplation of nature leads necessarily to the recognition of God.

56. Mathematics constitutes the needed starting point and guide in the study of the diversity of nature.

57. Mathematics should be treated physically, and mathematical forms and figures should be considered as the necessary outcome of an inner force acting from a center.

58. Language, the third element of education in correspondence with religion and nature.

59. Language, considered as primarily a complete organism, with its word elements bearing necessary relations to objects and attributes named.

60. The rhythmic law of language should be regarded in the early speech training of the child.

61. Writing and reading grow out of the self-active desire for expression, and should be taught with special reference to this fact.

62. Art and the appreciation of art constitute a general talent and should be provided for in the education of all youth.

63. The union of school and family influences essential to right education.
64. By the cooperation of home and school the right development of inner life should accompany the acquirement of external knowledge.
65. The unity of thought and purpose between parent and child may be maintained and strengthened during the school period.
66. The inner experiences and forces of mind and heart should be specifically cared for and developed.
67. Religious instruction should appeal to the immediate inner life rather than to hope of reward or fear of punishment hereafter.
68. Religious maxims should be memorized as expressing common experiences.
69. Direct training as to care of the body and use of the limbs is essential.
70. Physical training should involve in due time a knowledge of the bodily structure and a high regard for its true welfare.
71. The knowledge of things found in their local conditions and in their relations.
72. The first objects to be presented in the right course of instruction are the ones that are near and known as directly related to the child.
73. Every particular branch of instruction has its proper place of development from the earlier subjects of instruction.
74. In the study of plants, animals, etc., the work proceeds from particulars to generals, and again from generals to particulars in varied succession.
75. After the study of natural objects the works of man are to be presented.
76. From natural objects and the products of man's effort the study should proceed to include the relations of mankind.
77. The prime purpose throughout is not to impart knowledge to the child, but to lead the child to observe and to think.
78. The relations of nature and of life are to be interpreted largely through the medium of song and poetry.
79. So far as may be, the exercises of this class should grow out of immediate conditions and circumstances.
80. Observation lessons and language work, as pertaining to the affairs of ordinary life and as a basis of systematic science studies.
81. Development and culture come from work done rather than from ideas acquired.
82. By means of the several kindergarten gifts and occupations the constructive and formative faculties are to find expression.
83. Instruction in drawing begins with representation and comparison, and proceeds into invention.
84. Color work should deal with simple forms in pure and distinct colors.

85. Colors should be studied in their natural relations, in their differences and resemblances.
86. The right development of the color sense lifts man into a nobler moral atmosphere and adds interest to nature and life.
87. Spontaneous play is the outcome of vital energy and buoyancy and, under the guidance of the teacher, may be utilized in social development.
88. Stories and fables are necessary as furnishing a basis for the comparison of transient experiences.
89. The several ordinary branches of school study belong to a later period of education than do those modes of instruction already considered.
90. The general purpose of family and school instruction is to advance the all-sided development of the child and the complete unfolding of his nature.

From Friedrich Froebel's *The Education of Man*, translated by W. N. Hailmann. (N.Y.: Appleton, 1887), pp. 333 - 40.

Notes and References

Chapter One

1. Friedrich Froebel, *Autobiography*. (Syracuse, N.Y., 1889), p. 4.
2. *Ibid.*, p. 4.
3. Edward Wiebé, *Paradise of Childhood*. (Springfield, Mass., 1896), p. 14.
4. Froebel, *op. cit.*, p. 10.
5. Wiebé, *op. cit.*, pp. 16 - 17.
6. Froebel, *op. cit.*, p. 18.
7. *Ibid.*, p. 24.
8. *Ibid.*, p. 25.
9. *Ibid.*, p. 27.
10. *Ibid.*, p. 29.
11. *Ibid.*, p. 30.
12. *Ibid.*, p. 31.
13. *Ibid.*, pp. 36 - 37.
14. *Ibid.*, p. 38.

Chapter Two

1. Wiebé, *op. cit.*, p. 24.
2. *Ibid.*, p. 24.
3. Froebel, *op. cit.*, p. 59.
4. *Ibid.*, p. 60.
5. *Ibid.*, p. 60.
6. *Ibid.*, p. 61.
7. *Ibid.*, p. 77.
8. *Ibid.*, p. 78.
9. *Ibid.*, p. 78.
10. *Ibid.*, p. 79.
11. *Ibid.*, p. 81.
12. *Ibid.*, p. 85.
13. H. Courthope Bowen, *Froebel and Education Through Self-Activity*. (N.Y., 1897), p. 19.
14. R. H. Quick, "Friedrich Wilhelm August Froebel," *Encyclopaedia Britannica*, 11th ed. (Cambridge, England, 1910), v. 11, p. 239.

15. Wiebé, *op. cit.*, p. 31.

16. Jessie White, *The Educational Ideas of Froebel*. (London, 1907), p. 13.

Chapter Three

1. Wiebé, *op. cit.*, p. 33.
2. Froebel, *op. cit.*, p. 123.
3. *Ibid.*, p. 123.
4. *Ibid.*, p. 127.
5. *Ibid.*, p. 127.
6. Wiebé, *op. cit.*, p. 36.
7. *Ibid.*, p. 36.
8. *Ibid.*, p. 35.
9. *Ibid.*, p. 35.

10. Caroline D. Aborn, "Friedrich Froebel, Apostle of Childhood Education," *Childhood Education*, 13 (1937), p. 213.

11. *Ibid.*, p. 213.

Chapter Four

1. Alexander B. Hanschmann, *The Kindergarten System*. (London, 1897), p. 119.
2. *Ibid.*, pp. 122 - 23.
3. Froebel, *op. cit.*, p. 131.
4. *Ibid.*, p. 132.
5. Hanschmann, *op. cit.*, p. 131.
6. *Ibid.*, p. 133.
7. Wiebé, *op. cit.*, p. 39.
8. Hanschmann, *op. cit.*, p. 136.

Chapter Five

1. Frank Podmore, *Robert Owen, a Biography*. (London, 1906), p. 133.
2. *Ibid.*, p. 134.
3. Aborn, *op. cit.*, p. 212.
4. *Ibid.*, p. 214.
5. White, *op. cit.*, pp. 84 - 85.
6. Hanschmann, *op. cit.*, p. 146.
7. Emma W. White, "Frederic Froebel's Christian Kindergarten," *Catholic World*, 56 (1893), p. 509.
8. Aborn, *op. cit.*, pp. 214 - 15.
9. Frederick Mayer, *The Great Teachers*. (N.Y., 1967), p. 219.
10. Hanschmann, *op. cit.*, p. 159.

11. Jessie White, *op. cit.*, p. 85.

12. Frank P. Graves, *Great Educators of Three Centuries*. (N.Y., 1912), p. 225.

Chapter Six

1. Hanschmann, *op. cit.*, p. 177.

2. White, *op. cit.*, p. 114.

3. Matilda H. Kriege, *The Child; Its Nature and Relations*. (N.Y., 1877), p. 96.

4. William H. Kilpatrick, *Froebel's Kindergarten Principles*. (N.Y., 1916), p. 169.

5. *Ibid.*, p. 170.

6. *Ibid.*, p. 203.

7. *Ibid.*, p. 205.

Chapter Seven

1. Mayer, *op. cit.*, p. 216.

2. *Ibid.*, p. 217.

3. *Ibid.*, p. 217.

4. Friedrich Froebel, *The Education of Man*. (N.Y., 1887), p. 165.

5. *Ibid.*, p. 195.

6. Friedrich Froebel, *Pedagogics of the Kindergarten*. (N.Y., 1895), p. 62.

7. *Ibid.*, p. 94.

8. Berthe von Marenholtz-Bülow, *Reminiscences of Friedrich Froebel*. (Boston, 1877), p. 228.

9. Kilpatrick, *op. cit.*, p. 15.

10. *Ibid.*, p. 54.

11. Bowen, *op. cit.*, p. 93.

12. Mayer, *op. cit.*, pp. 220 - 21.

Chapter Eight

1. Irene M. Lilley, *Friedrich Froebel*. (Cambridge, England, 1967), p. 3.

2 *Ibid.*, pp. 3 - 4.

3. *Ibid.*, p. 4.

4. Froebel, *Education, op. cit.*, p. 168.

5. White, *op. cit.*, p. 43.

6. Froebel, *Education, op. cit.*, p. 151.

7. *Ibid.*, p. 151.

8. *Ibid.*, p. 152.

9. *Ibid.*, pp. 205 - 06.

10. *Ibid.*, p. 208.

11. *Ibid.*, p. 210.

12. *Ibid.*, pp. 224 - 25.

13. Bowen, *op. cit.*, p. 62.

14. Kilpatrick, *op. cit.*, p. 166.

14. Friedrich Froebel, *Letters on the Kindergarten.* (Syracuse, N.Y., 1896), p. 250.

16. Kilpatrick, *op. cit.*, p. 168.

17. Froebel, *Letters, op. cit.*, p. 123.

18. Kilpatrick, *op. cit.*, p. 186.

19. *Ibid.*, p. 187.

20. Friedrich Froebel, *The Mottoes and Commentaries of Friedrich Froebel's Mother Play.* (N.Y., 1895), p. xvii.

Chapter Nine

1. Marenholtz-Bülow, *op. cit.*, p. 36.

2. Hanschmann, *op. cit.*, pp. 132 - 33.

3. *Ibid.*, p. 130.

4. Wiebé, *op. cit.*, p. 55.

5. Marenholtz-Bülow, *op. cit.*, pp. 1 - 2.

6. Evelyn Lawrence, ed., *Friedrich Froebel and English Education.* (N.Y., 1953), p. 33.

7. Henry Barnard, ed., *Papers on Froebel's Kindergarten.* (Hartford, Conn., 1881), pp. 159 - 60.

Chapter Ten

1. Denton J. Snider, *The Life of Frederick Froebel.* (Chicago, 1900), pp. 428 - 29.

2. Marenholtz-Bülow, *op. cit.*, p. 198.

3. *Ibid.*, p. 199.

4. *Ibid.*, p. 199.

5. *Ibid.*, p. 200.

6. *Ibid.*, p. 201.

7. *Ibid.*, p. 202.

8. *Ibid.*, p. 202.

9. *Ibid.*, p. 202.

10. *Ibid.*, p. 203.

11. Robert Ulich, *A Sequence of Educational Influences.* (Cambridge, Mass., 1935), pp. 12 - 16.

12. Marenholtz-Bülow, *op. cit.*, pp. 256 - 57.

13. *Ibid.*, p. 264.

14. *Ibid.*, p. 203.

Chapter Eleven

1. Graves, *op. cit.*, p. 250.
2. Lawrence, *op. cit.*, p. 57.
3. Wiebé, *op. cit.*, p. 61.

Chapter Twelve

1. F. A. Cavanagh, "The Place of Froebel in Modern Education," in: Conference of Educational Associations, *Twenty-Seventh Annual Report* (London, 1939), pp. 200 - 7.
2. J. P. Slight, "Froebel and the English Primary School of Today," in: Lawrence, *op. cit.*, pp. 95 - 124.
3. Barbara Priestman, *Froebel Education To-day.* (London, 1946).
4. Kilpatrick, *op. cit.*
5. Graham Wallas, "A Criticism of Froebelian Pedagogy," in: the author's *Men and Ideas* (London, 1940), pp. 133 - 50. (Originally published in 1901).
6. *Ibid.*, p. 133.
7. Cavanagh, *op. cit.*, p. 200.
8. Kilpatrick, *op. cit.*, p. 201.
9. John Dewey, *Democracy and Education.* (N.Y., 1916), pp. 67 - 68.
10. P. Woodham-Smith, "History of the Froebel Movement in England," in: Lawrence, *op. cit.*, p. 91.
11. Dewey, *op. cit.*, p. 229.
12. *Ibid.*, p. 230.
13. O. B. Priestman, "The Influence of Froebel on the Independent Preparatory Schools of Today," in: Lawrence, *op. cit.*, p. 148.
14. Cavanagh, *op. cit.*, p. 207.
15. *Ibid.*, p. 207.
16. Woodham-Smith, *op. cit.*, p. 94.
17. Robert G. Kaiser, *Russia, the People and the Power.* (N.Y., 1976), p. 58.
18. Robert Ulich, *History of Educational Thought.* (N.Y., 1945), p. 291.

Selected Bibliography

PRIMARY SOURCES

The first collected edition of Friedrich Froebel's writings, *Gesammelte Pädagogische Schriften*, edited by Wichard Lange, in three volumes, was published at Berlin by Enslin in 1861-1862. The contents, as translated in Henry Barnard's *Kindergarten and Child Culture*, are as follows:

A supplementary list in H. C. Bowen's *Froebel* includes the following Froebel writings:

Thorough and satisfactory education for the deteriorating German character, the foundation and springhead needed for the German people. (1821.)

The Family Journal of Education. A weekly journal for the education of self and others. (Keilhau, 1826.)

Come, let us live with our children. A Sunday paper for like-thinkers. (1838-40.)

A large box of play and occupation for childhood and youth. Gifts 1-5.

Froebel's personally efficient work in Dresden and Leipzig, 1839; described by himself in fourteen letters to his first wife, and published by Dr. Lange in Nos. 2, 3, and 4 of the *Rheinische Blätter.* 1878. (A translation of these letters is appended to Miss Shirreff's *Short Life of Froebel,* published by Chapman & Hall.)

Froebel's Weekly Journal. A publication to serve as a link between all friends of human education. 1850. Edited by Dr. Lange at Hamburg.

Mutter- und Kose-lieder (Mother's Songs, Games, and Stories); for the generous fostering of child-life. A family book. Music by Robert Kohl, 1843. (Published for Dr. Lange by Enslin, of Berlin, 1866, 1874, 1878. Translated by Miss Dwight and Miss J. Jarvis, with introduction by Miss E. Peabody; Lee & Shepard, Boston. Also by Frances and Emily Lord; William Rice, London, 1885 and 1888.)

A Hundred Ball-songs for the games used in the Kindergarten of Blankenburg, 1843. (Music by Robert Kohl.)

A Journal for Friedrich Froebel's educational aims. Published by Froebel and his friends. Edited by Director Marquart in Dresden, 1851 - 52. Six numbers.

Froebel's letter to Kern, the teacher of the deaf and dumb in Eisenach, 1840.

Letter of Froebel's to the Rev. Dr. Felsberg, in Sonneberg, near Gotha.

Froebel's letters on the Kindergarten, 1838 - 52. Edited by Hermann Poesche and published in 1887; translated by E. Michaelis and H. K. Moore; Sonnenschein & Co., London. (Forty-one letters and four addresses to the women of Germany.)

Other English versions of Froebel's works are *Mottoes and Commentaries of Friedrich Froebel's Mother Play,* translated by Henrietta R. Eliot and Susan E. Blow (N.Y., 1909), and *Autobiography of Friedrich Froebel*, translated and annotated by Emilie Michaelis and H. K. Moore (Syracuse, N.Y., 1889). Selected writings are contained in Irene M. Lilley's *Friedrich Froebel, a Selection from His Writings* (London: Cambridge University Press, 1967), and *The Student's Froebel, Adapted from Die Menschener-ziehung of F. Froebel*, by William H. Herford (London, 1905, 2 v.)

SECONDARY SOURCES

BARNARD, HENRY, Ed. *Papers on Froebel's Kindergarten, with Suggestions on Principles and Methods of Child Culture in Different Countries, Republished from the American Journal of Education.* Hartford, Conn., 1881. The first and most comprehensive work dealing with Froebel and the kindergarten to be published in English; includes translations of many original works by and about Froebel.

BOWEN, H. COURTHOPE. *Froebel and Education through Self-Activity.* N.Y.: Scribner, 1897. Two biographical chapters are followed by detailed discussions of Froebel's writings and educational theories.

GRAVES, FRANK P. "Froebel and the Kindergarten." In the author's: *Great Educators of Three Centuries.* N.Y.: Macmillan, 1912, pp. 194 - 236. Traces early evolution of the kindergarten and summarizes Froebel's educational principles.

HANSCHMANN, ALEXANDER B. *The Kindergarten System, Its Origin and Development as Seen in the Life of Friedrich Froebel.* London: Swan Sonnenschein, 1897. An old but useful general biography, with full accounts of each stage of Froebel's career from birth to death.

KILPATRICK, WILLIAM H. *Froebel's Kindergarten Principles Critically Examined.* N.Y.: Macmillan, 1916. Examines Froebel's philosophy of education and views on kindergarten methods in the light of more recent practices and research.

LAWRENCE, EVELYN, Ed. *Friedrich Froebel and English Education.* N.Y.: Philosophical Library, 1953. Essays by six English educators on the growth of the Froebel movement in Britian; deals with the origin and history of the kindergarten in England, Froebel's influence on English primary and preparatory schools, and Froebel's educational and religious philosophy.

MARENHOLTZ-BÜLOW, BERTHE VON. *Reminiscences of Friedrich Froebel*, translated by Mary (Mrs. Horace) Mann. Boston: Lee & Shepard, 1895. A primary source, especially for the last years of Froebel's life, written by his leading disciple.

———— *The Child, Its Nature and relations; an Elucidation of Froebel's Principles of Education.* N.Y.: Steiger, 1872. Based upon the Baroness' close association with Froebel near the end of his career.

MEYER, BERTHA. *Aids to Family Government; or From the Cradle to the School, According to Froebel*. N.Y.: Holbrook, 1879. An interpretation of Froebel's teachings on all aspects of infant and kindergarten education, written by one of Froebel's students.

PRIESTMAN, BARBARA. *Froebel Education To-day*. London: Univ. of London Press, 1946. Detailed analyses of various aspects of Froebel's philosophy, viewed from the standpoint of modern applications and educational changes, especially in England.

SNIDER, DENTON J. *The Life of Frederick Froebel, Founder of the Kindergarten*. Chicago: Sigma Pub. Co., 1900. A general life, divided into three sections: Froebel as a youth, as a schoolmaster, and as founder of the kindergarten; wordy, ornate writing style, and only marginally useful.

WHITE, JESSIE. *The Educational Ideas of Froebel*. London: University Tutorial Press, 1907. An excellent short biography, covering the principal phases of Froebel's life and work.

WIEBÉ, EDWARD. *The Paradise of Childhood, a Practical Guide to Kindergartners, Including a Life of Friedrich Froebel, by Henry W. Blake*. Springfield, Mass.: Milton Bradley, 1896. A short general biography, followed by notes on the beginning of the kindergarten movement and separate discussions of each of Froebel's twenty "gifts."

Index